Bottoms Up!

by Gregg Kreutz

A Samuel French Acting Edition

SAMUELFRENCH.COM

ISBN 978-0-573-69207-9 Printed in U.S.A. #4195

To Shari Harper

MUSIC USE NOTE

Licensees are solely responsible for obtaining formal written permission from copyright owners to use copyrighted music in the performance of this play and are strongly cautioned to do so. If no such permission is obtained by the licensee, then the licensee must use only original music that the licensee owns and controls. Licensees are solely responsible and liable for all music clearances and shall indemnify the copyright owners of the play and their licensing agent, Samuel French, Inc., against any costs, expenses, losses and liabilities arising from the use of music by licensees.

IMPORTANT BILLING AND CREDIT REQUIREMENTS

All producers of *BOTTOMS UP!* *must* give credit to the Author of the Play in all programs distributed in connection with performances of the Play, and in all instances in which the title of the Play appears for the purposes of advertising, publicizing or otherwise exploiting the Play and/or a production. The name of the Author *must* appear on a separate line on which no other name appears, immediately following the title and *must* appear in size of type not less than fifty percent of the size of the title type.

Bottoms Up! was first performed August 3, 1989 at the Brooke Hills Playhouse, Wellsberg, West Virginia, Sharon Harper, Managing Director and Paula Welch, Producer; under the direction of Gregg Kreutz, with set design by Crystal Motto and with the following cast:

THE PORTER .... James Matterer
SEÑORA VALDEZ .... Bev Brady
JUNE SHERWOOD ....Cathie Barger
SMITH.................................Neil Nixon
TONY SCOPEC.......................... Tim Eckard
VICTORIA .... Peggy Barki
GEORGE RUSHMORE.................Rich Ivaun
KEITH.................................Keith West
RAYMOND PUMPHREY ....Rick Call

CHARACTERS

The Porter
Señora Valdez
June Sherwood
Raymond Pumphrey
Smith
Tony Scopec
Victoria
George Rushmore
Keith

The action takes place in the Hotel Grande on the Caribbean island of Santa Pequeña.

ACT I

Morning

ACT II

Immediately following

ACT I

SCENE: The set is two floors of the Hotel Grande, a slightly run-down establishment on the Caribbean island of Santa Pequeña. The main floor lobby is on the Left side of the stage and on the Right, a couple of feet higher, is the second floor hallway and room 203. The decor is aggressively tropical, with bamboo, rattan, and nautical paraphernalia scattered about. The lobby side of the stage has an Upstage entrance and a Stage Left entrance. On the Upstage Left side of the lobby is a large stand with a sign over it saying SCUBA. Swimming equipment, inner tubes, life vests, and so on, cover the stand. It is recommended that behind the stand, out of the audience's view, there be a small exit. Also on the stand is a radio, and there is a wall phone nearby. A hassock sits Downstage Right, and Downstage Left is an open window. Next to the window, Downstage, is a wall hanging made of woven bamboo that's in the shape of a large lizard.

There are two ways of getting from the lobby to the second floor. One is the elevator, which needs a hidden operator inside to open the doors and move the floor indicator. The other is the stairs. Using them entails walking down a few steps off the Downstage edge of the stage, going over to another set of steps, Stage Right, and climbing up to the hall. During the climb, some extra marching around in circles will strengthen the illusion that the distance between two floors is being covered.

At the Upstage end of the hall is the door to Rushmore's room. Downstage from there, on opposite sides of the hall are doors to the elevator (Stage Left) and to June's room (Stage Right). In June's room is a bed, a skirted vanity, an Upstage high shelf for a radio, a bathroom door, and a large window. Between the window and the bathroom door, on the Upstage wall, is another bamboo lizard. This one large enough to be partially hidden behind. June's bed must be high enough to crawl under, light enough to lift, and strong enough to jump on.

Finally, the play requires two identical, snap-lid suitcases.

AT RISE: As the LIGHTS come up, island MUSIC is heard and the PORTER enters from Upstage. HE is a free spirit; larcenous in a friendly sort of way and slightly crazy. HE is carrying a tray and moving to the rhythm; dancing through the lobby looking for drink glasses. HE finds one on the scuba stand, picks it up, sips from it and, puts it on this tray. HE sees a glass sitting on the hassock, dances over, picks it up, and is starting to exit Stage Left when He stops. HE is suddenly realizing what was sitting beside the hassock: an unattended suitcase. HE goes back and, after looking around furtively to make sure he is unobserved, picks it up. HE lifts it to his ear and shakes it. Very discreetly, HE begins exiting Stage Left with the suitcase when ...

SEÑORA. (*Entering with JUNE from Upstage. SEÑORA VALDEZ is a proud, opinionated woman who is aggressively protective of what's hers.*) Ah, look! Look who has found it. Our own porter. You see! There was no need to worry.

JUNE. Oh, that's wonderful! (*SHE goes to the porter and takes the suitcase.*) Oh, thank you so much. (*JUNE is guileless and wholesonely pretty. She has an innocent's firm sense of justice.*)

PORTER. It was nothing.

SEÑORA. He is so modest. You see, there is no need to worry at the Hotel Grande. Your bags are always safe. (*To Porter.*) Gracias.

PORTER. Gracias, Señora.

SEÑORA. He is a fine porter. A wonderful porter.

(*PORTER is smiling happily.*)

SEÑORA. Those who say he is not are completely wrong.

(*PORTER makes an angry face.*)

SEÑORA. If they would only talk to him they would know this. Don't you think?

JUNE. Well, getting to know people really does help you understand them.

SEÑORA. I do not speak of those who are guests here, but of others. Other people. *They* do everything to my porter they can. Everything!

JUNE. Oh, dear. What do they do?

SEÑORA. Do? Well, they say things about him. They accuse him. They make accusations.

(*PORTER makes a sad face.*)

SEÑORA. It is not right. Do you know what it is?

JUNE. Wrong?

SEÑORA. It is jealously. (*SHE rubs his head.*) He is *too* good a porter. (*Shifting into a business-like mood.*) Now. June. You will be in room 203 and we need to know if you wish the bathroom to have cold *and* hot water.

JUNE. Well, if it's not too much trouble.

SEÑORA. The trouble does not matter. If you wish cold and hot, you get cold and hot! (*To Porter.*) You hear?

(*To June.*) Don't worry about trouble. (*To Porter.*) Room 203. She wants cold and hot.

PORTER. Si, Señora. (*HE exits with a discreet but longing glance at the suitcase.*)

SEÑORA. Oh, what a porter! Now you have your suitcase I can show you a little more of our hotel.

JUNE. It certainly is a very beautiful place.

SEÑORA. Of course is beautiful. Como no? The Hotel Grande is very beautiful. It maybe is not the most modern hotel in the world, but it is so full of history and tradition. Everybody who comes to this island want to stay here.

JUNE. I bet they do. I sure did. The brochure had such a nice picture of it, sitting up on this cliff, silhouetted against the tropical sky. I just fell in love, and I'm so glad you had a room available.

SEÑORA. Yes, you are very lucky. Everyone want to stay here. They know the hotel is not only beautiful, but is also respectable. I insist on this. Only respectable people can stay here. People like you.

JUNE. Oh, thank you.

SEÑORA. I look at you, I know I see someone who is full of innocence and dignity. Am I right?

JUNE. Well, I hope so.

SEÑORA. Respectability! You are full of it! I know these things! I have a deep inner sense about people. I see you, I see your gracefulness, I also know you are an artist. Am I right?

JUNE. Well, really, I'm more of a teacher.

SEÑORA. Just as I thought. What kind of teacher?

JUNE. I teach aerobics.

SEÑORA. Oh, my heart is touched. How selfless. You teach aerobics. What do you teach them?

JUNE. It's an "it," not a "them." It's a movement kind of thing.

SEÑORA. Ah, movement! How wonderful! Oh, such talent! I love talent. (*SHE leads JUNE to the elevator.*) You see our elevator. It goes all the way to the top.

JUNE. It's very nice.

SEÑORA. Then it comes down.

JUNE. I'm glad.

SEÑORA. I could say to guests, "Use the stairs, climb the stairs over here. (*SHE shows June the stairs.*) Save electricity." But our guests are too respectable. Too respectable. We have a dignified business man from the important city of Cleveland, Ohio.

JUNE. I'm from Ohio.

SEÑORA. Ah-ha! Exactly! I knew I was right about you! (*SHE leads JUNE to the phone.*) You see the telephone? It is known as lobby phone. You call any room in the hotel from here. It's very modern. Up-to-date. The types who stay here demand up-to-date. Important people. All important.

JUNE. That's great.

SEÑORA. (*Confidentially.*) We have movie-makers staying at the hotel.

JUNE. Really?

SEÑORA. I am so in love with culture. These movie-makers wanted to stay here, what could I say? I love art. I love the film.

JUNE. Me too.

SEÑORA. I can see this about you. I know people. I have a special sense. In here, in my stomach. My stomach tells me who is to be trusted. There is ...

SMITH. (*Offstage.*) Señora! Señora Valdez!

SEÑORA. (*Calling out to him.*) I am here. (*To June.*) Now you will see. This is the businessman I spoke of. From Cleveland. (*Calling out.*) I am in the lobby.

(*SMITH enters. HE is a suspicious looking character wearing a dark suit, black shirt, white tie, and sunglasses. His coolness is easily undermined.*)

SMITH. (*To Señora.*) Oh, great. There you are. Bueno. I need your help. I'm trying to track down your porter.

SEÑORA. Ah! Then is perfect that you come in here now! You will see the porter when he returns and you can meet the new guest, my new friend, June Sherwood.

SMITH. (*Removing his shades with a flourish.*) Very pleased to make your acquaintance. Any friend of Señora Valdez is a friend of mine.

SEÑORA. (*To June.*) The perfect gentleman. Did I not tell you? (*To Smith.*) Miss Sherwood is a dancer.

JUNE. Actually, I'm not really a dancer. I really teach aerobics.

SEÑORA. (*Confidentially to Smith.*) An "it" not a "them."

SMITH. You don't say.

JUNE. And actually, it's really not aerobics. Strictly speaking, it's my own special kind of exercise that develops the inner and outer person that I created myself.

SEÑORA. An inventor!

JUNE. Sort of.

SEÑORA. We want to hear everything about it!

JUNE. Really? Everything?

SMITH. Sure. More or less.

JUNE. (*Rapidly.*) O.K. Well, you see, I believe being fit isn't just a physical thing. It also has to do with, you know, behavior, and so my system emphasizes honesty and integrity as vital exercise components. I think you need to take whatever's sagging and down in your life, whether it's your hips or your values, and firm them up.

SEÑORA. This is so true.

JUNE. So I named my program ... (*Counting off the acronym letters on her fingers.*) Bio Organic Tension Taming Original Movement System Stressing Upright Principles. Or, for short, Bottoms Up.

SMITH. Catchy.

JUNE. Thank you.

SMITH. So, ah, what's the deal with you being here? You giving classes on the island?

JUNE. Hopefully. You see, I was teaching my system at this health club in Toledo and they had a lot of management problems that kept getting worse and suddenly the whole place went kerpluee.

SEÑORA. It blew up!?

JUNE. Financially speaking.

SEÑORA. Oh, how tragic. Was anybody killed?

JUNE. Well, you see, it was a bankruptcy problem. So there I was, cleaning out my locker, kind of wondering what to do with myself, when I look down and, guess what was lying there on the exercise mat?

SEÑORA. A body?!

JUNE. No, a brochure for this hotel that somebody had left. Just lying there.

SEÑORA. It was fate!

JUNE. I picked it up and saw all these beautiful pictures of this hotel.

SEÑORA. I tell you it was fate. (*To Smith.*) Yes?

SMITH. Sounds like fate.

JUNE. That's just what I thought. It's like something was saying to me, "Go to Santa Pequeña and stay at the Hotel Grande." That's how I live my life. I try to be alert to the messages around me. That's part of what Bottoms Up is all about. Learning to be attuned to what's around you and trying to be always totally honest with yourself.

SEÑORA. (*To Smith.*) She always sees the truth about other people.

SMITH. (*Jokingly.*) She does? In that case I got to go. (*HE laughs until he realizes the joke is too true to be funny. Then awkwardly ...*) Well, I don't mean "in *that* case." In any case I got to go. Anyway. Anyhow look what's happened to the time.

SEÑORA. What?

SMITH. It's gotten later. I got to talk to the porter. Don't worry, I'll find him. It was a pleasure. (*HE exits stage Left.*)

SEÑORA. What a gentleman! And I know this the moment I see him. I feel these things.

(*PUMPHREY, looking exhausted from a morning of hotel hunting, enters from Upstage. HE is a cynical worrier suspicious of the unfamiliar. HE's conservative in attitude and dress and wears a bow tie. HE leans against the scuba stand. SEÑORA notices him and leads JUNE out of his hearing range.*)

SEÑORA. Like that man over there. I look at him. My stomach feels very funny. He is not a person of dignity.

JUNE. Gee, he looks dignified. Maybe your stomach is making a mistake.

SEÑORA. No, is never wrong. (*To Pumphrey.*) May I help you?

PUMPHREY. I hope so. (*HE accidentally knocks a mask to the floor.*) I've been having a terrible time. (*Picking it up.*) Things are falling apart. I need a room very badly!

SEÑORA. (*To June.*) What did I tell you? (*To Pumphrey.*) Are you wanting to be a guest here?

PUMPHREY. Yes, I am! Every other place is filled up.

SEÑORA. You have tried to stay at other hotels?

PUMPHREY. Well, ah ... not very successfully. I've been running around this island all morning. Do you have any rooms?

SEÑORA. We do. Yes. But you should know that we are selective about ...

PORTER. (*Entering.*) Señora! Señora! Una problema. Una problema major!

SEÑORA. So many problemas! Excuse me. Permisso. (*Aside to June.*) Please keep an eye on this man. (*SHE exits with Porter.*)

JUNE. (*Walking up to Pumphrey.*) Hi there. My name is June Sherwood.

PUMPHREY. Hello. I'm Raymond Pumphrey. Do you think that woman is going to give me a room?

JUNE. Oh, I think so. I'm sure she will.

PUMPHREY. Thank goodness! Whew! What a relief! What a morning! (*Looking around distastefully.*) What a hotel!

JUNE. I know. I loved it the moment I saw it. The second I walked in here I felt like I kind of belonged. (*Suddenly.*) Wait a second! Could you do me a big favor?

PUMPHREY. Well, ah ... I suppose if there's really ...

JUNE. Could you take a picture of me? Like of me arriving here at the hotel for the first time?

PUMPHREY. Aren't we a little late for that?

JUNE. I know. But my arrival could turn out to be an important moment in my life. We can recreate it. I'd love a photographic record. Would you mind? (*SHE gives him the camera.*)

PUMPHREY. (*Pleasantly resigned.*) Where are you going to stand?

JUNE. (*Going to the Upstage entrance.*) I'll be coming in the door and looking around for the first time. You stand over there.

PUMPHREY. All right. I'm not very good with cameras. Are you ready?

JUNE. No, wait. I want to make myself look like I'm seeing the lobby for the first time. (*SHE strikes a dramatic pose and makes a manic-looking grin.*)

PUMPHREY. It's just my opinion, but I think it would be better if you *didn't* look like you're being electrocuted.

JUNE. (*Modifies slightly.Through her grin.*) Better?

PUMPHREY. Much better. Now. Ready? Set? ... Hold *it.* (*HE flashes the picture.*) Good. Very nice. A very moving reenactment. Anything else I can document for you?

JUNE. No, thanks. (*SHE is given the camera.*) Why don't I take a picture of you?

PUMPHREY. Me? There's no need for that. I don't think my lobby-reaction pose is up to your standards. I might look unenthusiastic. (*Cupping his hand to his mouth for a mock stage whisper.*) I'm not totally delighted with Santa Pequeña.

JUNE. You're not? And after you've come all this way? That must be disappointing.

PUMPHREY. No. I knew I'd be unhappy if I came here and now that I'm here, sure enough, I'm unhappy.

JUNE. Well ... why are you here?

PUMPHREY. Good question.

JUNE. (*Pleased.*) Thank you. (*Pause.*) What's the answer?

PUMPHREY. It's complicated.

JUNE. Yes?

PUMPHREY. I live in Scranton, Pennsylvania.

JUNE. Uh-huh?

PUMPHREY. And I teach chemistry at Scranton Community College, and they've gotten an endowment to sort of broaden the outlook of the faculty; you know, expand their point of view. All of us, at least once, have to go on a trip.

JUNE. How nice.

PUMPHREY. And the worst part is, we don't get to pick where we go. They decide.

JUNE. What countries do they pick?

PUMPHREY. Countries like this. (*HE sits down on the hassock.*) They love to send their faculty to remote, emerging nations that haven't emerged much. Underdeveloped countries. Places where high-tech is a toilet that flushes. I can't believe I'm here.

JUNE. Come on now, cheer up. I just love Santa Pequeña. Well, so far, at least. See if you can guess why I'm here.

PUMPHREY. You're being punished for something.

JUNE. No. Come on, I'll give you a hint. (*Does a subdued version of her aerobics dance with a lot of arm.*)

PUMPHREY. Ah ... you're a travelling juggler?

JUNE. No. (*SHE continues dancing.*)

PUMPHREY. Um ... um ... You've come to be cured of a strange nervous disorder.

JUNE. No. (*Still dancing.*)

PUMPHREY. O.K. I give up. Why are you here?

JUNE. Aerobics.

PUMPHREY. There's a lot of aerobics here?

JUNE. There may not be any.

PUMPHREY. That's the first good thing I've heard about this place.

JUNE. No, it's not good. Aerobics balances the system.

PUMPHREY. So you're going to teach everyone to balance their systems?

JUNE. I think so. I hope so. It's a little vague in my mind. I'm really sort of taking directions from, well, I guess I could call it my inner voice.

PUMPHREY. And your inner voice said to come here?

JUNE. Uh-huh. (*SHE drifts over to the window.*)

PUMPHREY. If I were you, I'd have my inner voice checked.

JUNE. (*Looking out the window.*) I absolutely can't believe this view! I mean, look how high up we are! It's amazing! I'll bet it's a forty-foot drop to the rocks down there.

PUMPHREY. (*Rising.*) I won't be here long enough to test it.

JUNE. How long will you be here?

PUMPHREY. That's the trouble. They told me the next plane out isn't till tomorrow morning.

JUNE. But you only got here today. Don't you want to learn about Santa Pequeña's culture?

PUMPHREY. Just the part between here and the airport. The college says I have to come here, but they don't need to know how long I stay.

JUNE. And you don't want to stay?

PUMPHREY. No. You see, *my* inner voice doesn't like me to leave the United States. (*HE cups his hand over his ear and pretends to listen.*) Ooo, hold it. I'm hearing something. Make that the greater Scranton area.

JUNE. You don't ever want to see new things?

PUMPHREY. Not unless I've seen them before.

JUNE. But that seems so ... so limited.

PUMPHREY. Careful. I love limited.

JUNE. Aren't you interested in learning about different kinds of people?

PUMPHREY. Well ... no. You see in a place like this difference can create tension and of course tension can then lead to unfriendly sorts of things.

JUNE. Like what?

PUMPHREY. Oh like short tempers, resentment, rudeness, guerrilla warfare, terrorism, kidnap ...

JUNE. Now that's silly. The cab driver told me that Santa Pequeña has had one president for a very long time and there hasn't been any trouble for years.

PUMPHREY. Exactly my point; a powder keg. Did you get a look at the porter? Did you see his face? He's mad. He hates us! To him we're the enemy.

(*The PORTER enters unseen by Pumphrey.*)

PUMPHREY. I mean, if looks could kill we'd be ...

PORTER. Senorita.

(*PUMPHREY jumps in the air.*)

PORTER. Do you wish me to take the bags to your room?

JUNE. No, that's all right. Leave them here for now. I'll go up in a few minutes.

PORTER. As you wish. (*HE exits.*)

PUMPHREY. See what I mean?

JUNE. No, what?

PUMPHREY. Didn't you notice his hostility?

JUNE. He didn't seem hostile.

PUMPHREY. He had a contemptuous manner.

JUNE. He didn't seem contemptuous.

PUMPHREY. Well, not overtly. But, come on. I mean, he *said,* "Do you wish me to take the bags to your room?" but he *meant,* "Come the revolution—" (*HE draws his finger across his throat.*)

JUNE. He didn't mean—(*SHE draws her finger across her throat.*) You're being paranoid.

PUMPHREY. I'm not paranoid, I'm realistic. That porter is seething.

JUNE. (*Dismissively.*) Oh ...

PUMPHREY. What we have just seen, for all intents and purposes, is a seething porter.

JUNE. Now he is no such thing. You're getting upset over nothing. You can't go around projecting all this negativity on innocent people. (*Snapping her fingers.*) Wait a second. I've got a very good idea. This is an important idea.

PUMPHREY. What is it?

JUNE. I think you should *talk* to the porter.

PUMPHREY. Talk to the porter? What about?

JUNE. Well, just get to know him. Understand him. See the world from his point of view. Right now you're fearing him. Wait here, I'll go get him. (*SHE starts to leave.*)

PUMPHREY. No, wait! Stop!

JUNE. I don't mind. (*SHE continues leaving.*)

PUMPHREY. Really! Don't go! *Stop!*

(*SHE stops.*)

PUMPHREY. June ... ah ... I'm sure you mean well, but I very much don't want to engage in a personal encounter with the porter.

JUNE. But don't you think ...

PUMPHREY. I have quite a strong feeling about this! So thank you anyway and ...

(*SEÑORA enters.*)

JUNE. Señora Valdez. I'm so glad you're here. I think you can clear something up. My friend here that I just made, Mr. Pumphrey ...

PUMPHREY. Raymond Pumphrey. Nice to see you again. But look, everything's fine. I'm sure that ...

JUNE. Mr. Pumphrey here thinks the porter is a threatening person, and since you were saying that getting to know peop ...

SEÑORA. He what!? He says he was threatened!?

PUMPHREY. (*Trying to smile pleasantly.*) I didn't say that! That isn't what I said!

JUNE. No, he didn't exactly say *he* was threatened. I just meant ...

SEÑORA. (*To Pumphrey.*) You! You would insult my porter! Who would never hurt a fly?!

PUMPHREY. I didn't insult him. I'm sure he's an exemplary person. He just has a certain demeanor.

SEÑORA. Now you go too far! He does not have a demeanor! He is a wonderful porter!

PUMPHREY. I can see that now. Yes.

SEÑORA. No!

PUMPHREY. No?

SEÑORA. No. He is more than a porter!

PUMPHREY. I'm sure he is.

SEÑORA. Much more than a porter!

PUMPHREY. No question about it.

SEÑORA. He is ... (*With a dramatic flourish.*) ... MY NEPHEW!

PUMPHREY. You must be very proud.

SEÑORA. He has overcome so many problems. People like you accusing him. All his life. Saying he is strange. Saying he takes things. But I know better! I listen to my stomach. You don't!

PUMPHREY. I don't.

SEÑORA. I don't listen to people like you. People who say he is crazy.

PUMPHREY. I didn't say he was crazy!

SEÑORA. You come to my hotel. No reservations. You fiddle the scuba. You snoop around.

PUMPHREY. I'll clear that up right now. I was not scooping ... sooping ... stoopi ... (*To June.*) How could you do this?

SEÑORA. See, I knew he was not respectable. I am tempted to call the police! (*SHE goes to the phone.*) Where are you from?

PUMPHREY. (*Following her.*) Scranton. Scranton, Pennsylvania. I teach at Scranton Community College. Here! Look! Here's my card! See?

SEÑORA. (*Taking card.*) I am tempted to write to them and say you have insulted an innocent person. That you have been unfriendly to people of Santa Pequeña.

PUMPHREY. No! No! Don't write to them. Look, it's a misunderstanding.

SEÑORA. (*Begins running around lobby.*) Raoul! Raoul!

PUMPHREY. (*Following her.*) Listen, there is absolutely no need to call Raoul.

(*The exchanges get quicker and louder.*)

SEÑORA. Raoul!

PUMPHREY. Please don't go bothering ...

SEÑORA. Raoul!

PUMPHREY. Really, you don't need to call Raoul!

SEÑORA. RAOUL!

PUMPHREY. (*Screaming.*) DON'T CALL RAOUL! (*Pause.*) Who's Raoul?

SEÑORA. He is the porter, my nephew. I want to tell him what you said.

PUMPHREY. I didn't say anything. This is all ... (*To June.*) Why did you ? ...

SEÑORA. Raoul!

PUMPHREY. (*To June.*) Tell her! Tell her I was just making an observation!

JUNE. He really didn't mean to offend anyone or slander ...

SEÑORA. Slander! It is slander!

(*PORTER enters.*)

SEÑORA. Raoul! Did you threaten this man?

PORTER. This man? No. Who is this man?

PUMPHREY. Hi. I'm Raymond Pumphrey. (*HE shakes Porter's hand.*) It's a real pleasure. Heard a lot about you.

SEÑORA. Now you would try to be friends. It is too late for that. You cannot stay in my hotel.

PUMPHREY. What?! You've got to let me stay here. All the other hotels are full.

SEÑORA. You should think of that before you assassinate his character.

PUMPHREY. This isn't fair. June!

JUNE. Señora Valdez, he really didn't mean any harm and I didn't mean any harm and I would hate for him to not be able to stay 'cause I brought up his remarks. (*SHE is almost weeping.*)

SEÑORA. (*Comforting her with an embrace.*) There, there. I'm glad you told me what he said. That's good. Don't be upset.

PUMPHREY. (*Trying to join the hug.*) We're all just going to completely forget the whole thing.

SEÑORA. (*Scaring hin* away.) Away! Get away! You have done enough!

JUNE. Couldn't he stay?

SEÑORA. No, it is impossible.

PUMPHREY. Well, if you won't let me stay, then ... I'm going to leave! Somebody must have a room somewhere. (*HE exits.*)

JUNE. (*Calling after him.*) Goodbye, Stanley. I'm sorry.

PORTER. (*Waving cheerfully.*) Goodbye.

SEÑORA. Here! You come to the desk and we will register you.

(*JUNE and SEÑORA exit. The PORTER again tries to make off with the suitcase. This time, HE picks it up and starts down the stairway, but is interrupted by ...*)

SMITH. (*Entering from Upstage.*) Porter? Porter?

PORTER. (*Putting the suitcase on one of the stairs.*) Si? You want me?

SMITH. Yeah. I want to talk to you. You speak English?

PORTER. (*Joining Smith.*) Si.

SMITH. Good. You're going to need a lot of it in the next few days. Tell you what I'm going to do. I'm going to give you some money. Just give it to you. No strings. O.K.? You want the money?

(*The PORTER nods eagerly.*)

SMITH. 'Course you do. Why do I want to give you money? (*SMITH puts his hand on Porter's shoulder.*) Let's just say I like you.

(*PORTER nuzzles his head affectionately against Smith's hand.*)

SMITH. No no no. (*Retracting hand.*) Let's put it another way. Somebody is arriving here in the next few minutes. Somebody important. A big guy. A certain big guy from Cleveland. No, forget that. Let's not say where he's from. Let's just say he's a very important man. A venture capitalist. He may be from Cleveland, maybe he's not. Who can say?

PORTER. Who?

SMITH. Let me tell you something about this man.

PORTER. Yes?

SMITH. I am his, shall we say, business associate.

PORTER. Business associate.

SMITH. And because he's so important, I don't want him to have any, what you might call problems. You with me?

PORTER. No problems.

SMITH. (*Handing him the money.*) That's why I'm giving you this twenty bucks. So that we won't have any problems. Scopec hates problems.

PORTER. Scopec?

SMITH. Let's say I didn't say Scopec. Pretend the name Tony Scopec was not said.

PORTER. (*Cheerfully wagging his head back and forth.*) O.K. I pretend. Scopec is famous man?

SMITH. (*Laughing modestly.*) You don't control 13% of every bookie along central Lake Erie without gaining a certain, shall we say, repute.

PORTER. Repute. You guard this man?

SMITH. In a manner of speaking.

PORTER. You are a bodyguard?

SMITH. I like to say I'm in the personal security field.

PORTER. You are armed?

SMITH. I might be.

PORTER. I *know* you don't have a gun.

SMITH. As a matter of fact, I do.

PORTER. No. Is impossible.

SMITH. Sorry, amigo, I got one.

PORTER. No.

(*The exchanges increase in speed and volume.*)

SMITH. Yes I do.

PORTER. No you don't.

SMITH. Look, pal, I know whether I got a gun or not.

PORTER. You don't have a gun.

SMITH. I do!

PORTER. You don't.

SMITH. I do!

PORTER. You don't.

SMITH. I've got a gun!! (*Pulls his gun out.*) Here! What do you call this?!

PORTER. (*Pause.*) That's not a gun.

SMITH. What do you mean, it's not a gun?! What are you talking about?

PORTER. It looks like a gun, but it's not. It doesn't work.

SMITH. Of course it does!

PORTER. Here. I show you. (*HE takes the gun.*) Look. Is broken. I will fix it. (*HE starts heading for the Upstage exit.*)

SMITH. Stop!

PORTER. Is no problem. No problema. I fix your gun good as new. (*HE runs off Upstage with gun.*)

SMITH. Stop! Hold it! Wait! Give that back! (*HE starts after Porter.*)

(*SCOPEC enters from Stage Left carrying a suitcase identical to June's. HE is a big man with a short fuse and a tendency to solve problems with physical force.*)

SCOPEC. Smith!! What are you doing?! What's the matter?!

SMITH. Nothing's the matter.

SCOPEC. No slip-ups? You know I hate slip-ups.

SMITH. So far so good.

SCOPEC. Where are you going?

SMITH. I didn't tip the porter.

SCOPEC. Don't worry about the porter. You got bigger problems. I got bigger problems. And having to work with you is probably the biggest.

SMITH. Is that the money in the suitcase?

SCOPEC. Quiet! Jesus! That's what I'm talking about. You don't know how to do things. (*HE grabs Smith by the lapels and, in a stage whisper says:*) When somebody is transporting eight months' worth of tax-free capital gains, don't say, "Is that the money in the suitcase?"

SMITH. (*In a strangled voice.*) O.K. I won't.

(*SCOPEC releases him.*)

SMITH. Is it?

SCOPEC. (*Grabbing him again.*) Yes! Now be quiet about it. The whole idea of a laundry operation is secrecy. Don't broadcast it. This is serious money. You understand?

SMITH. Yeah. I do.

SCOPEC. And we brought it here to *quietly* reprocess it. That's what this island is good for.

SMITH. I think you're right. I mean, I know you're right. You're right. That's why I was thinking that instead of sending all of it through some account here, we could break it up and get some of it over to a different account, maybe on some other island, and use ...

SCOPEC. Listen to me, DON'T THINK!

SMITH. But I think ...

SCOPEC. (*Grabbing him.*) No. that's what I don't want you to do. You always come up with an extravaganza when a simple deal would be better. Now this is a simple deal. We've brought the money into Santa Pequeña, and now all we have to do is get it into one of those banks that Sal explained about. So I'm going to check that out. and I want you to stay here in the lobby with this suitcase and not think.

SMITH. How about if I took the suitcase to the hotel safe and had ...

SCOPEC. (*Grabbing him and sitting him down on the pouf with the suitcase.*) Don't have ideas! Understand! I want this suitcase to stay here in this lobby. Can you handle that?

SMITH. Yes.

SCOPEC. Say it!

SCOPEC. Suitcase in lobby. Suitcase in lobby. No problem.

SCOPEC. I'll be right back. (*HE exits.*)

(*The PORTER enters.*)

SMITH. Hey you! Where's my gun!? I want it returned!

PORTER. Oh, the gun. You want the gun back.

SMITH. Of course, I want the gun back. Give it to me.

PORTER. (*Retreating.*) Now I am so busy. Busy busy busy. I can't help you now! (*HE exits Upstage.*)

SMITH. Hold it! Hold it right there! You better come back here! (*SMITH, clutching the suitcase, starts to tear off after him, but is held back because of Scopec's suitcase-lobby instructions. HE starts and stops a few times, then takes the suitcase and tucks it behind the scuba stand. HE exits, running after the porter.*)

SCOPEC. (*Enters from Stage Left, looks around, and doesn't see Smith or the suitcase.*) What the hell!?

(*HE looks around some more and sees June's suitcase on the stairs. HE picks it up and gets to the middle of the lobby with it when SMITH enters.*)

SCOPEC. What are you? A moron? What the hell were you thinking of, leaving the suitcase just sitting here!?

SMITH. (*Puzzled.*) I hid it.

SCOPEC. I'll make a note of that. Something else you're bad at is hiding things. Where the hell were you?!

SMITH. Oh well, I had a problem that I needed to work out. But I just left for a second.

SCOPEC. That's too long! You don't leave money lying around like that! Come with me!

(*THEY exit with the suitcase, Upstage. SEÑORA and JUNE enter from Stage Left.*)

SEÑORA. There. Now you are all signed in. You are now an official guest.

JUNE. Well, thank you. I'm really happy, but I feel bad about Mr. Pumphrey. I feel so responsible.

(*RUSHMORE comes out of his room and gets on the elevator. HE is avidly mercenary and a shameless self-promoter. His manner is grand and theatrical.*)

SEÑORA. No. He was not right for the Hotel Grande. I am glad you spoke up. From now on, whenever you have a problem, you speak to the responsible people. The people in charge. O.K.?

JUNE. O.K. I will. I just hope he finds another ... that's funny, one of my bags is missing again. I'm sure I put it down right over there.

SEÑORA. The yellow suitcase?

JUNE. (*Looking around.*) Yes.

SEÑORA. That bag is always trying to sneak away. (*SHE looks around.*) Always running off. (*To bag.*) Where are you? Where are you hiding? Come out now. Don't be shy. (*SHE looks behind the scuba stand; to bag.*) I see you.

You can't hide from Señora Valdez. (*SHE picks up the bag and gives it to June.*)

JUNE. I don't know how it got over there, but thank you again. (*SHE pushes the elevator button.*)

SEÑORA. I am always happy to help our guests.

(*The door opens and RUSHMORE steps out as JUNE steps in.*)

JUNE. See you later. (*The door closes.*)

SEÑORA. Ah, Mr. Rushmore.

RUSHMORE. Ah, Señora Valdez. Buenos dias. It looks like another lovely day in Santa Pequeña.

SEÑORA. Yes. This is perfect weather for making movies? Yes?

RUSHMORE. Yes. Very good filming weather. Hope to get some footage in the can today. I'm having a bit of trouble locating our leading lady, however. Have you seen her?

SEÑORA. No, I haven't seen her today. Yesterday I saw her.

RUSHMORE. I see.

(*THEY are moving towards the Stage Left entrance.*)

SEÑORA. She is such a lovely person. Is she a *famous* movie star?

RUSHMORE. Not quite yet, but we have high hopes for her. Especially if she will be a little more cooperative about the costume situation.

SEÑORA. There are certain things she won't wear?

RUSHMORE. (*Stepping aside so that SHE can exit first.*) It's more that she insists on wearing certain things.

(*SEÑORA exits.*)

RUSHMORE. (*To himself, as HE takes one last look around the lobby.*) Like clothes. (*Exits.*)

(*JUNE gets off the elevator on the second floor, goes to room 203, opens the door with her key, goes in and looks around. SHE does a modified aerobics dance, then goes into the bathroom.*

RUSHMORE enters the lobby with VICTORIA. SHE is a full-figured, attractive actress with a fiery personality.)

RUSHMORE. Now come on back here, Victoria. Come on! What are you doing?

VICTORIA. I'm leaving. Goodbye.

RUSHMORE. You can't leave!

VICTORIA. Oh, yes, I can! The deal is off. I am not going to be in your movie.

RUSHMORE. But ...

VICTORIA. It's over, Kapootsky.

RUSHMORE. Let's talk about it.

VICTORIA. No!

RUSHMORE. Try to be analytic. Let's isolate the negative, confront it and purge it.

VICTORIA. It's all negative. This film is the pits. It's disgusting. It's exploitive. I won't do it.

RUSHMORE. O.K. I'm starting to sense where some of the problem area is.

VICTORIA. The whole thing is a problem area. It's cheap. It's vulgar. It's amateurish. Everything is fifth-rate. I'm not going to take my clothes off in this production.

RUSHMORE. Didn't the title give you any clue as to what sort of a movie we were making? I think you should have expected nudity would be required in a film called *Tan All Over*.

VICTORIA. That wasn't what you called it when you signed me up.

RUSHMORE. Right. Then it was called *Birthday Suit.*

VICTORIA. Whatever it was called, I was led to believe this was a professional project.

RUSHMORE. It *is* professional.

VICTORIA. Well, I think you *need* a professional in the lead. A professional hooker!

RUSHMORE. Isn't that redundant?

VICTORIA. You're redundant. You're redundantly dumb.

RUSHMORE. That's a little presumptuous.

VICTORIA. Presumptuous! Here you've spent the last twenty-four hours trying to get me to perform with nothing on but coconut oil, and you complain about me being presumptuous. I'm leaving.

RUSHMORE. You can't leave. We have a contract.

VICTORIA. I never signed it. Remember, you didn't have any copies. I should have been suspicious about this operation when you couldn't raise the money to have a Xerox made.

RUSHMORE. Well, what am I supposed to do? I've got my crew all ready.

VICTORIA. Oh, come on. You can't call one teenager with a video camera a crew.

RUSHMORE. It's a streamlined crew.

VICTORIA. Goodbye. I'm going to the airport now and fly out of here.

RUSHMORE. Who am I going to replace you with?

VICTORIA. (*Shoving him out of the way.*) Go to the police station and look through their indecent-exposure files. (*SHE exits.*)

(*KEITH enters. HE's a laid-back guy in his late teens who seeks the path of least resistance. HE's dressed in island clothes and is carrying a video camera. HE's looking over his shoulder at the Stage Left exit.)*

KEITH. Hey, where's "the chest" going?

RUSHMORE. She's leaving.

KEITH. Why?

RUSHMORE. She had all sorts of reasons, but I'm sure you constantly calling her "the chest" played its part.

KEITH. I didn't call her that all the time.

RUSHMORE. That's true. Sometimes you called her "Miss Bazoongas."

KEITH. But what about the movie? She's the star. In fact, she's the whole show unless you count the coconut oil.

RUSHMORE. Oh, I'm upset. This is a catastrophe! Actresses! They are an endless source of frustration. You think they're going to behave like responsible, decent people, and the next thing you know they won't take all their clothes off. Start saying things like, "I studied acting so that I could act, not show everyone my body."

KEITH. I mean, why do they think it's called show business?

RUSHMORE. Exactly. It's getting harder and harder to put together a project these days. You try to get a little quality, somebody like Victoria arrives, and she won't do the job. And, Keith, you know why she won't do the job?

KEITH. She has standards?

RUSHMORE. Wrong. We don't have enough money. If this was a full-scale Hollywood, big budget production, she'd be naked as a jay-bird. It's money, Keith, cash, green stuff, lettuce.

KEITH. Oh, speaking of lettuce, you said you'd pay me today.

RUSHMORE. You disappoint me, Keith. Don't you understand what I'm saying? I'm underfunded. I lack capital. You don't need money, I need money.

KEITH. How about tonight?

RUSHMORE. Keith, we have a crisis on our hands. Our star has walked off the set. I need a new star, or all that I've invested goes down the drain.

KEITH. Would tomorrow morning be ...

RUSHMORE. (*Angrily.*) Enough! Enough! Later I'll pay you. When I get some money and an actress. (*Looking into the distance, as if seeing a vision.*) What I need is an uninhibited personality, a child of nature, a free spirit, a ...

KEITH. A slut?

RUSHMORE. Exactly. Let's both work on it. I'm going back up to my room and see what I can come up with over the phone.

KEITH. And I'll hunt around here. Maybe this hotel has some free spirits in residence.

(*KEITH exits and RUSHMORE gets on the elevator. SCOPEC enters from the Upstage entrance dragging SMITH along by the head. HE is in a rage.*)

SCOPEC. You're dead Smith! Dead! You blew it! All you had to do was watch the suitcase.

SMITH. O.K. O.K. I know. You're right. You're absolutely right. (*SCOPEC plants him on the hassock. Timidly.*) But I do feel that when we opened the suitcase, you shouldn't have, you know, gotten so angry about it. I think you got a little too angry.

SCOPEC. I'm funny that way. I get upset when I'm expecting cash and finding hair curlers.

SMITH. Right, but in my opinion it seemed to me that what you did was a little too excessive. I think it's fair to say it was an over reaction to hurl the suitcase off the cliff. Now we got a problem about trading to get it back.

SCOPEC. No. You got a problem! You get it back!

SMITH. O.K. I can do it. I met this girl. It won't be too bad. I just need to plan a strategy.

SCOPEC. No! Don't plan any strategies. Just get the suitcase. You don't need a big production. Just get it. And get it now!

SMITH. All right. I'll call her room. Make sure she doesn't open anything. And then I'll explain things; well, not too many things. I'll give her a story.

SCOPEC. Nothing fancy!

(*RUSHMORE gets off the elevator and goes into his room.*)

SMITH. No, a nice simple story. Look, there's the phone. I'll call and there won't be anything to worry about. (*Picks up the lobby phone receiver.*) Hello. Yes, ah, buenos dias to you, too. What I need is for you to connect me to a lady's room. (*Pause.*) No. Room of a lady. A certain lady whose name is June and I'm not sure of her last name. O.K. That sounds right. Room 203? Good. (*Aside to Scopec.*) See, this isn't so bad.

SCOPEC. Just get the suitcase.

(*June's PHONE rings.*)

SMITH. It's ringing.

SCOPEC. And keep it simple.

JUNE. (*Coming in from the bathroom and picking up the phone.*) Hello?

SMITH. Hello, June. We just met a little bit ago. I'm the one you described your aerobics to. Do you remember?

JUNE. Oh, yes, from Cleveland.

SMITH. Right. Wherever. June, there's been a mistake. Well, not a mistake so much as a mix-up. Sort of an interesting thing, really. It turns out that the suitcase you've got really belongs to what we might as well call ... me.

JUNE. Oh no. It's mine.

SMITH. Well, I know it looks like yours, but it's really mine.

JUNE. Hold on a second. I'll look inside and prove it.

SMITH. (*Panicked.*) No, wait! Don't do that! Stop! Don't open the suitcase!

JUNE. I'm sorry, but why not?

SMITH. Because ... because ... Well, to be frank, I, or I should say me and my partner work for the United States government. In a secret capacity. And that suitcase—the contents of that suitcase is—are confidential

JUNE. Here's the thing; if this isn't my suitcase, why don't you just bring up my suitcase and we'll trade.

SMITH. That is a good idea. Really a good idea, but there's a problem with it. You see ... ah ... we took your suitcase because we needed to run a check on you for security purposes.

JUNE. Why?

SMITH. Why? Because we ... have decided to use you as a cultural exchange representative of our country. We want you to teach aerobics to the islanders here in Santa Pequeña.

(*SCOPEC, now seated on the hassock, buries his head in his hands.*)

JUNE. Me? Really?

SMITH. That's right. You. Congratulations.

JUNE. But when do I start? What do I do? I feel sort of unprepared.

SMITH. Don't worry about a thing. We'll explain everything to you. In fact, I'll come up now and explain things and get the suitcase, and so on.

JUNE. But it's so weird that you would all of a sudden pick me to teach the people here about aerobics.

SMITH. I was frankly very impressed with your attitude. It seemed very ... impressive, and then after we did the security check on your suitcase, we ...

JUNE. I don't mean to sound like I'm not appreciative, but now that you've security-checked my suitcase, couldn't I get it back?

(The PORTER enters from Upstage, carrying a drink tray. At first neither HE nor the MEN see each other.)

SMITH. I'm sorry. You will get it back, but right now it's being sent to Washington.

JUNE. Well, this is just the most amazing thing. I just can't believe it, Mr. ... Mr. ... What is your name?

SMITH. (*Suddenly seeing the Porter.*) Porter!!

(The PORTER sees him and runs back Off Upstage.)

SMITH. Porter!

JUNE. Mr. Porter?

SMITH. Who?

JUNE. You're Mr. Porter?

SMITH. Ah ... Why not. Yes. I'm Mr. Porter and you're June and I'll come up to your room now and get the suitcase and, ah ... brief you and so on. O.K.?

JUNE. O.K. Great!

SMITH. And, June ...

JUNE. Yes?

SMITH. Welcome aboard.

JUNE. Thank you. Goodbye. (*SHE hangs up, and during the following dialogue, puts the suitcase under the bed and goes into the bathroom.*)

SMITH. (*Hangs up.*) There. (*Walking over to Scopec.*) We're all set.

SCOPEC. (*Grabbing Smith by the tie.*) I told you to keep it simple!

SMITH. It was simple. Sort of. In a way.

SCOPEC. It was dumb. Now she thinks she works for the U.S.Government!

SMITH. What's wrong with that?

SCOPEC. She starts blabbing, people get interested and then they check us out. They got an American Embassy here full of agency people. And they get paid to mess up laundry operations like ours.

SMITH. Come on. She isn't going to call the embassy. I don't think. (*HE pushes the elevator button.*)

SCOPEC. Smith, pay attention; if she contacts anybody about us, you are through. Understand?

SMITH. Yeah, I do.

SCOPEC. Good.

(*HE exits as the door opens and SMITH gets on.*
The PORTER enters wearing a tool belt with a toilet plunger. During June's telephone call, HE takes the stairway up to the second floor.
The PHONE rings.)

JUNE. (*Picking it up.*) Hello? ... Oh, hello, Raymond. O dear ... I know ... I just feel awful about what happened. Especially after you took my picture and everything. I can't believe it got so terrible. I hope you're not just too upset with me ... Oh, you are. Well, Raymond, I am so sorry. I certainly hope you got some other accommodations ... Oh, you didn't. Uh-huh. Well, sure you could drop by. Yes, well, I'm in room 203.

(*The PORTER arrives at her door and KNOCKS.*)

JUNE. Oh, hold on a second. Someone's at the door. Hello?

PORTER. Porter. I come to fix your water.

JUNE. Come on in. (*SHE lets him in.*)

PORTER. I need to open the pipe in the bathroom.

JUNE. O.K., help yourself.

PORTER. Gracias, senorita. (*HE goes into the bathroom.*)

JUNE. (*Into the phone.*) They're giving me cold and hot. But, Raymond, guess what!? Something wonderful has happened. I have been selected to be part of a cultural exchange program ... Yes ... Isn't it amazing? Teaching my system. The United States Government has hired me ... I know! I'm so happy! Well, O.K., see you later. (*SHE hangs up.*)

(*SMITH gets off the elevator, goes up to June's room, hesitates a moment, and then KNOCKS.*)

JUNE. Who is it?

SMITH. It's the man you met in the lobby. The suitcase man, you know, the government person.

JUNE. Mr. Porter?

PORTER & SMITH. (*Together; with PORTER sticking his head out of the bathroom.*) Yes.

JUNE. (*To Porter.*) Sorry. I was talking to someone out here.

PORTER. O.K. (*Disappears into bathroom.*)

JUNE. (*Opening her door.*) Hi! Oh, this is wonderful! I can't believe it. I simply can't believe it! Come on in.

SMITH. (*Entering.*) Thank you.

JUNE. Don't thank me. I mean, I'm so grateful to you.

SMITH. Yes, well, don't mention it. (*HE starts looking around in a simulated casual manner, trying to see the suitcase.*) Yes, this is a nice room. Kind of small. Not too small. Not too big, though. No danger you're going to get lost in here. (*A strained laugh while HE looks for the suitcase.*) Doubt if you could lose the suitcase in here. (*Another laugh.*)

JUNE. Nope. Not much chance of that. This is so terrific. You see, I was thinking maybe this was a bad idea to come here to Santa Pequeña, and then you called.

SMITH. That's right, I sure did. Is the, ah, suitcase around here?

JUNE. It sure is. To think that when I met you before, I thought you were a businessman from Cleveland, and now it turns out you're a government official from ... where are you from?

SMITH. I'd rather not say. Where did you put the ...(*HE's still looking.*)

JUNE. A government official who'd rather not say! How thrilling! I don't think I've ever met a government official before. Unless you count mailmen. And a tax auditor I once ...

SMITH. (*Desperately.*) Where is the suitcase?

JUNE. I put it under the bed.

(*SMITH drops to his knees, pulls out the suitcase and puts it on the bed just as the PORTER enters.*)

PORTER. It is all fixed. I am all done.

SMITH. (*Suddenly seeing Porter.*) You! Stop right there!

JUNE. Me?

SMITH. Him.

PORTER. Here?

SMITH. Yeah, right there. I want to talk to you. Miss Sherwood?

JUNE. Call me June, Mr. Porter.

PORTER. (*Affectionately.*) June.

SMITH. Not you, me. June?

JUNE. Mr. Porter?

PORTER. Yes?

SMITH. Me!! She's talking to me! (*Going up to the Porter and holding him by the arm.*) And I want to talk to you.

(*The PORTER is struggling.*)

SMITH. June, I have some cultural attaché sorts of things I need to talk to the porter about. I hope you'll excuse us. And don't do anything while I'm gone like, ah ... for instance ... don't unpack.

JUNE. O.K.

(*SHE goes into the bathroom. SMITH and PORTER go into the hall, SMITH shutting the door behind them.*)

SMITH. Give me back that gun!!! Do you hear me?!

PORTER. Yes I do. You say, "Give me back that gun."

SMITH. Give it to me!

PORTER. Why?

SMITH. 'Cause it's mine.

PORTER. (*Groaning as if in pain.*) Oh ...

SMITH. What the hell's the matter?

PORTER. I'm so sad. I don't have anything.

SMITH. You're going to have even less if you don't give back that gun. Comprende?

PORTER. I don't even have a wallet.

SMITH. Oh, these people! Listen, pal, you're making a big mistake fooling around with someone like me. Back in Cleveland, I walk into a bar, everybody looks nervous. If you were smart, you'd look nervous too.

PORTER. I am nervous. I'm nervous because I don't have a wallet.

SMITH. Goddammit! If I give you a wallet will you give me that gun?

PORTER. What kind of wallet?

(*SCOPEC enters the lobby and gets on the elevator.*)

SMITH. I don't know, a wallet that's like mine. Like this. (*HE pulls out his wallet.*) Listen, I can't fool around about a wallet out here. I got important business in there. Give me the gun.

PORTER. (*Moaning.*) Wallet!

SMITH. All right, all right. Now give me the gun and I'll go buy you a wallet. A wallet like mine.

PORTER. No, I want a good wallet.

SMITH. This is a good wallet. What do you think? Look, it's genuine eelskin.

(*The exchanges get faster and louder.*)

PORTER. No, it's not.

SMITH. Of course it is. This is real eelskin.

PORTER. It's not.

SMITH. It is too!

PORTER. It's not.

SMITH. Yes it is!

PORTER. No it's not.

SMITH. Don't tell me it's not!!

PORTER. It's not. Here, I show you. (*HE takes the wallet and studies it.*) You see, eelskin is softer and ... Oh, excuse me, I hear the bell. (*HE starts running off.*) The bell is ringing. I must go. Porter duties. (*HE runs down the stairs with the wallet.*)

SMITH. Give that back! Stop! Now! Give it back! (*HE starts after the Porter, but is halted by ...*)

SCOPEC. (*Getting off the elevator.*) Smith! What's happening? Where are you going?

SMITH. Oh ... I ... er ... Porter. I got to settle things with the porter.

SCOPEC. Don't worry so much about the porter. Is everything going O.K.?

SMITH. Like clockwork.

SCOPEC. Where's the aorta woman?

SMITH. Aerobics. She's in there. I was just talking to her, and then the porter ...

JUNE. (*Opening her door.*) Oh, there you are. Can I unpack yet?

SCOPEC & SMITH. No!

SMITH. No. Can we come in?

(*THEY enter.*)

SMITH. I want to introduce you to the cultural attaché general.

JUNE. I'm really honored.

SCOPEC. Where's the suitcase?

JUNE. Now don't you worry. It's over there.

SCOPEC. Get it, Smith.

SMITH. Porter.

SCOPEC. Whatever. Just get the suitcase and let's get out of here.

JUNE. Excuse me, but don't you want to brief me on what I'm going to be doing here in Santa Pequeña?

SMITH. We sure do. But now isn't that good a time.

SCOPEC. Yeah, it's a bad time.

JUNE. Yes, but ...

SCOPEC. Smith, get the suitcase.

JUNE. (*Blocking his path.*) Just tell me a *little* bit about what you have planned. I mean, if anybody asks, I want to be able to tell them something.

SCOPEC. Wrong, lady. We don't want you telling anybody nothing.

SMITH. Or nobody anything.

SMITH. (*Leading her Downstage.*) You see, it's important that you keep in mind the sensitive nature of this mission.

JUNE. Except I can't help but wonder: Why is teaching aerobics sensitive?

SMITH. June, this situation here is very explosive. Very, very explosive.

JUNE. The aerobics situation?

SMITH. (*Putting finger to lips.*) Sh ... Let me explain. Physical fitness when used correctly—notice I said when used *correctly*—is good for the body, the mind, and the country. But as you well know, if it's misused ...

JUNE. Yes?

SMITH. If it's misused, ah, ... ah ... Poof, chaos. Suddenly you get a lot of irresponsible people running around in sweat suits.

JUNE. And that's bad?

SCOPEC. Of course it's bad. Who needs a lot of irresponsible, sweaty people?

JUNE. So my assignment has been a secret?

SMITH. Yes, and we have to know that it is staying a secret. You didn't, how shall I put it ...?

SCOPEC. Squeal.

SMITH. That's right. You didn't, as we say in the foreign service, squeal?

JUNE. Well, I did kind of tell this one person.

SCOPEC. Who?

JUNE. This man I met in the lobby. I just spoke to him on the phone.

SCOPEC. And what did you tell him?

JUNE. Well, kind of everything.

SCOPEC. (*To Smith.*) I told you this was a stupid idea. (*To June.*) You shouldn't have told anybody.

JUNE. Well, I'm terribly sorry, but, well ... after all, everyone's going to know soon when I start demonstrating tummy toning.

SMITH. That's true, but in the area of cultural exchange the key element is surprise.

SCOPEC. That's right. That's the big element. Now about the suitcase here ...

JUNE. I'm afraid I don't understand. Why is surprise important?

SCOPEC. Don't worry about it.

JUNE. Well, it just seems funny that I would ...

SCOPEC. Lady, listen. I don't want to say this twice. Don't worry about anything, and keep your mouth shut.

JUNE. Well, I don't think ...

SCOPEC. (*Violently.*) Or somebody's going to shut it for you!

JUNE. How dare you! How dare you! How dare you speak to me like that!

SMITH. Listen, June, this is ... don't be offended. He didn't mean any harm, did he, did you?

SCOPEC. I just don't like a lot of jabbering.

JUNE. Well, you can just leave, then! I don't care if you *are* Cultural Affairs Attaché General! I want you to go away!!

SMITH. June. Calm down. The general here has been under a lot of stress and ...

JUNE. I have gotten all excited about showing people how to combine uplifting principles with exercise and then you two come up here and harass me! (*SHE sits on the bed and cries.*) Just go away.

SCOPEC. Yeah, let's get out of here. Get that suitcase and ...

JUNE. No, don't take anything.

SMITH. But I know you know that suitcase is U.S Government property.

JUNE. I don't care. I think you have been very disrespectful, and I don't want to give you anything! (*SHE puts the suitcase on her lap and clutches it.*)

SMITH. Well, you have to give us that.

(*KEITH enters the lobby and gets on the elevator.*)

JUNE. No!

SCOPEC. Lady, you're going to give us that suitcase or ...

JUNE. No! No! No! (*SHE jumps off the bed with the suitcase, goes to the phone and picks it up.*)

SCOPEC. (*Approaching her.*) Give it to me!

JUNE. (*Into phone.*) Hello. Could you connect me to the American Embassy? (*To Smith and Scopec who have frozen in their tracks.*) I believe in always talking to the appropriate people and I'm going to find out who they are and tell them all about you and your rude behavior. They should be informed about the sorts of people that are ...(*Back into the phone.*) O.K. Thank you.

SCOPEC. Smith!

SMITH. Porter. June, there's no need to be calling the embassy. No need at all. Really. That could jeopardize the whole ... ah ... situation.

JUNE. Well, you two had better go, then.

SMITH. But what about the aerobics program? What about cultural exchange? (*Poignantly.*) What about tummy toning?

JUNE. I'll demonstrate tummy toning when you two can demonstrate good manners. If you don't leave right now I'm going to tell the embassy all about your conduct.

SCOPEC. Listen, I'm not putting up with this kind of ...

JUNE. (*Into the phone.*) Hello! Hello! American Embassy? Yes, I'm calling because I'm having a problem with the attitude of ...

SMITH. Look! It's not a problem!

SCOPEC. (*To Smith.*) You better stop her!

JUNE. (*Into the phone.*) There are two cultural exchange repres ...

SMITH. There is no problem! You can hang up!

JUNE. Not unless you leave.

SCOPEC. (*To Smith.*) I warned you about this!

SMITH. June, there is no need for ...

JUNE. (*Back kinto the phone.*) ... and one of them has been very ...

SMITH. O.K. Look. We're leaving. (*HE leads SCOPEC to the door.*) See! Watch! (*HE opens the door.*) We're going out the door, so don't bother the embassy any more about us, O.K.?

JUNE. O.K. You go, I'll hang up, and then I'm going to do some aqua pressure stress reduction.

SMITH. Gonna what?

JUNE. Take a shower. I just really want you to leave me alone. (*Into the phone.*) Not you. Them.

SMITH. (*As HE gets SCOPEC out the door.*) Us and we understand. We want you to be in a good frame of mind for the program. So everything's fine.

(*KEITH gets off the elevator.*)

SMITH. You can just relax and don't open the suitcase while we're gone and don't forget to hang up and remember that basically there are no problems. (*HE shuts the door.*)

SCOPEC. Smith, you got problems!

JUNE. (*Into the phone.*) Thanks anyway. Goodbye. (*SHE hangs up, puts the suitcase out of sight under the skirted vanity and goes into the bathroom.*)

(*KEITH, standing by Rushmore's door, is unseen by the MEN. HE listens to what follows with increasing interest.*)

SMITH. Don't worry, Mr. Scopec. This is just a temporary setback. The money is safe. Let's leave her alone now. I promise you this will clear up soon. I do think you were a little rough on her.

SCOPEC. Well, it's my money! I get to be rough on her.

SMITH. You know, as far as she's concerned, she's here for some intense physical activity with a lot of natives.

SCOPEC. I don't care about that. She's just a money-mover. All this (*HE does awkward imitation of aerobic bump and grind that looks obscene.*) huffing and puffing crap is irrelevant to me. I mean, who cares?

SMITH. She does. Remember, that's her job. She's a professional.

SCOPEC. (*Seeing Keith by the elevator door.*) Hey, kid, hold that elevator.

(*KEITH pushes the door button and SCOPEC and SMITH get in the elevator.*

The instant the door closes, KEITH excitedly knocks on Rushmore's door.)

KEITH. (*KNOCK KNOCK.*) Hey, George. Open up.

RUSHMORE. (*Opening the door.*) Oh, Keith. Listen, I can't get anyone. I've just been calling New York, and every actress there is either busy or has heard about me.

KEITH. Don't worry. I think I've got the solution. Come on. Step out here. I have found her! Guess where she is?

RUSHMORE. Where?

KEITH. In that room right there.

RUSHMORE. You're kidding.

KEITH. No. You want someone with experience,right? No more Suzy Squeamish. Someone who won't mind a little, ah ... frontal and backel.

RUSHMORE. That's right, and she's next door? Did you ask her?

KEITH. No.

RUSHMORE. How do you know she'll frontal and backel?

KEITH. I heard these two men come out of her room. They were talking about her. I think she's, how you say, in the love business.

RUSHMORE. You're kidding. What does she look like?

KEITH. That's the problem. I don't know. I haven't seen her.

RUSHMORE. I'll tell you what, if she looks like anything, I'll use her. But Keith, let's get some fanfare going. Go talk to her and tell her how important I am in movies and everything, and set it up so she'll be excited to do it. O.K.?

KEITH. Super.

RUSHMORE. Knock on my door when you're done. (*RUSHMORE goes into his room.*)

KEITH. Check. (*KEITH goes to her door and knocks. KNOCK KNOCK.*) Hello.

JUNE. Who is it?

KEITH. Hello. It's Keith.

JUNE. (*Opens door.*) Hi. Who's Keith?

KEITH. (*Stepping into the room.*) It's not so much who I am, but who I work for. I am the assistant, the right-hand man, the aide-de-camp of George Rushmore.

JUNE. I'm very pleased to meet you. (*Pause.*) Who is George Rushmore?

KEITH. I guess you've been a little cut off from V.I.P. news lately? Been a little out of touch?

JUNE. I don't know. Maybe.

KEITH. George Rushmore is only the premiere American director on this island.

JUNE. Oh, the American director. And is he involved in cultural activities?

KEITH. Cultural activities? Well, yes, you could say that.

JUNE. Oh, this is a great relief to me. I was so worried that the people who just left were the only, you know, men I was going to be dealing with.

KEITH. Those two? (*HE gestures towards the door.*) Yes, well, you're going to like Mr. Rushmore so much more. He has a whole philosophy about people and art and he feels that the body is a musical instrument that needs lots of care and attention and oiling. And he lives that philosophy.

JUNE. What a wonderful point of view for a representative of our country.

KEITH. (*Slightly confused.*) That's just how I feel.

JUNE. It's so unstuffy, so unremote.

KEITH. George Rushmore is very unremote. He's really what you'd have to call a hands-on director.

JUNE. Oh, am I ever relieved.

KEITH. And the project he and I are developing here is dynamic, it's physical, but tastefully so, and what we'd like to know is if you're ready to jump on board.

JUNE. Ready and eager!

KEITH. I like that attitude. Now I've got a surprise for you. I bet you can't guess where Mr. Rushmore is staying. I bet you can't.

JUNE. The American Embassy?

KEITH. Interesting guess. No, he's staying right next door to you. Room 201. Right here. I'll go get him.

JUNE. O.K. Let me get straightened up. (*Goes into the bathroom.*)

KEITH. (*Knock on Rushmore's door. KNOCK KNOCK.*) Hey, George, everything's cool.

RUSHMORE. (*Opening the door.*) Is she cute? Is she willing?

KEITH. Jackpot.

RUSHMORE. Fantastic. Keith, you're a champ. And you did a good PR job?

KEITH. She loves you already.

RUSHMORE. Wonderful! I want you to go down to the bar and get yourself a piña colada and put it on my bill.

KEITH. Gosh. Thanks, George. (*HE gets on the elevator.*)

(*RUSHMORE KNOCKS on the door.*)

JUNE. Who is it?

RUSHMORE. George Rushmore.

JUNE. Oh, come in. I am so glad to see you.

RUSHMORE. Believe me, I am even happier to see you.

JUNE. The last two men really were very upsetting.

RUSHMORE. Well, I suppose you get that every now and then.

JUNE. But honestly, I came here ready to work and suddenly the people from whom I most expect a gentle sort of handling, all of a sudden ...

RUSHMORE. It's just terrible. And let me assure you right now that none of that sort of thing will occur while you work with me. I believe gentleness is ultimately the most stimulating.

JUNE. That's right. It stimulates you to do a better job.

RUSHMORE. Precisely.

JUNE. And I won't have to be with those two men again?

RUSHMORE. Absolutely not!

JUNE. Oh, I'm so happy. You see, I think you're a much better representative of your country.

RUSHMORE. If only others thought as you do.

JUNE. Your assistant told me a little bit about what you believe in and, well, I think it's very beautiful.

RUSHMORE. We try. You know, some people think my projects are too open, too liberated, too concerned with the physical.

JUNE. Oh, but I think the physical is so important.

RUSHMORE. So you don't mind being involved?

JUNE. Mind? I am thrilled! It's my life. I love working with people and the more the better.

RUSHMORE. And you don't mind being in a ... natural state?

JUNE. Not at all. Of course, I don't think this is so much a state as a country.

RUSHMORE. Right. But I mean, you don't have any reservations about ... ah ... physical activities?

JUNE. Look, that's what I get paid for.

RUSHMORE. Wonderful. Now before we finalize this, I guess I should ask you to, you know, show me a little of , ah ... actually, a lot of what we're going to see.

JUNE. I'll be glad to. Would you ... ah ... (*SHE gestures, indicating that he should turn around.*)

RUSHMORE. (*Turning his back to her, facing Downstage.*) Oh, I see, very effective, a nice reserved beginning.

JUNE. (*Has lifted off her dress, revealing a head-to-toe exercise suit.*) O.K. Ready.

(*RUSHMORE turns around. JUNE is doing her strange exercise movements.*)

RUSHMORE. Ah-ha. Well, that *is* nice. Mmmm. Very effective. Now if I could just interrupt for a moment. Just for a moment ... STOP!!

JUNE. (*Stops.*) What is it?

RUSHMORE. I was thinking I was going to see more of what was going to happen on the project.

JUNE. Oh ... you want me to do a little more of what I do.

RUSHMORE. That's right.

JUNE. O.K., but you're going to have to join in.

RUSHMORE. Well, I'm not sure right now is a good ...

JUNE. Mr. Rushmore, I believe in total involvement, full participation.

RUSHMORE. Are you sure you want to?

JUNE. I want to be there for as many people as possible and really help them work up a sweat.

RUSHMORE. But right here? Right now?

JUNE. When better? I know. I'll turn on some music.

RUSHMORE. I really don't think ...

JUNE. Come on now, loosen up! (*SHE turns her back to Rushmore as SHE turns on the radio.*)

RUSHMORE. All right! I don't want anyone saying George Rushmore is inhibited. (*HE starts undressing.*)

JUNE. (*Her back still to him.*) That's right. Stay open and loose.

RUSHMORE. (*Getting his pants off.*) You're certainly a welcome change from who I was working with before. She was so uninterested in interaction.

(*The MUSIC comes on.*)

JUNE. There! Now we can ... (*SHE turns around and sees Rushmore.*) Mr. Rushmore! What are you doing?

RUSHMORE. Taking my clothes off?

JUNE. My goodness! That isn't really necessary.

RUSHMORE. It's not?

JUNE. Don't take any more off, please. O.K., now, just feel the rhythm inside you and keep up with me. (*SHE is doing stretching exercise movements to the music.*)

RUSHMORE. What?

JUNE. Keep up with me. Move! Arms up! Head back. Jump in rhythm! Up! Up!

RUSHMORE. This isn't really ... (*HE is reluctantly joining in.*)

JUNE. Come on. You're slowing down.

(*PUMPHREY enters the lobby from Upstage. HE is tiptoeing to the elevator.*)

RUSHMORE. This is a more athletic preliminary than I'm used to.

JUNE. Up! Up! Keep it up!

RUSHMORE. I'm trying!

(*The movements are getting more exaggerated, and RUSHMORE's reluctant efforts are looking more awkward.*

SEÑORA enters from Stage Left and sees the unsuspecting Pumphrey.)

JUNE. Now come on!

(*THEY'RE both dancing wildly.*)

JUNE. No quitting! This is for everyone. Young, old, male, female.

RUSHMORE. Very generous of you, but ...

JUNE. Let's go! Off to the side. Stretch. Spin around.

(*THEY are facing Upstage.*)

JUNE. O.K. Bend. Bend. Bottoms up.

(*RUSHMORE and JUNE are bending over. RUSHMORE is holding his back in pain.*)

RUSHMORE & SEÑORA. STOP!

(*EVERYBODY freezes.*)

CURTAIN

ACT II

The action is continuous.

SEÑORA. What are you doing!?

RUSHMORE. Could we turn that off?

JUNE. O.K. (*SHE goes to the radio and turns it off.*)

PUMPHREY. I'm just dropping by. Visiting. Hoping you'll give me a room?

SEÑORA. No. I will not have slanderers staying in the hotel.

PUMPHREY. I am not a slanderer.

RUSHMORE. I've got to go to my room. I'm expecting a call.

JUNE. A call?

SEÑORA. You called him names.

RUSHMORE. A call from the coast.

PUMPHREY. I did not call him names.

SEÑORA. You did!

JUNE. You don't want to see anymore?

PUMPHREY. Please!!

SEÑORA & RUSHMORE. NO!!!

RUSHMORE. No. Maybe later. Right now I've got to get to my room.

PUMPHREY. Just a little room?

SEÑORA. You can not stay here. This is final.

JUNE. See you later. Goodbye.

SEÑORA. Goodbye.

RUSHMORE. Goodbye.

PUMPHREY. Goodbye?

(During the following conversation, a now exhausted RUSHMORE goes out the door, shuts it, and leans against the doorframe before staggering into his room. JUNE goes into the bathroom.)

PUMPHREY. Señora, it was all a misunderstanding. You can ask June. She knows it was a mistake. It was really because of her that this confusion came about.

SEÑORA. Oh!! Now you would drag innocent people into your situation.

PUMPHREY. I'm not dragging anybody anywhere. I know, I'll pay extra!

SEÑORA. You would try to bribe the owner of Hotel Grande?

PUMPHREY. It's not a bribe. (*Whimpering.*) I just need a place to stay.

SEÑORA. You can not stay here! This is final. I will instruct the porter to see you out. (*SHE exits but can be heard yelling ...*) Raoul! Raoul!

(PUMPHREY anxiously goes to the elevator and pushes the button. HE hears ...)

PORTER. (*Offstage.*) Oh, si, Señora. No problema.

(PUMPHREY, suddenly panicked and trying to hide, backs against the elevator as the PORTER enters from Upstage. The PORTER is carrying the wallet and gun. As HE wanders to the middle of the lobby, HE scratches his head with the gun barrel. PUMPHREY reacts in growing horror as the PORTER backs up towards him until HE is standing, without realizing it, right in front of Pumphrey; the person he was sent to find. Not seeing him anywhere, the PORTER wanders over to look behind the scuba stand. PUMPHREY uses that

moment to dash to the stairs and tear up them. The PORTER, unable to find Pumphrey, exits.)

PUMPHREY. (*KNOCKING at June's door.*) June! Quick! Open up! June! June! June!

(*HE is KNOCKING and looking around and doesn't notice JUNE opening the door. HE knocks against air and stumbles into the room.*)

PUMPHREY. Oh, hello, June.

JUNE. Hello, Raymond. You look frazzled. What's the matter?

PUMPHREY. Things haven't been working out very well at all! This is the only hotel with vacancies, and I not only can't get a room, but I've got gun-wielding porters hunting for me!

JUNE. I'm sure you're exaggerating.

PUMPHREY. I'm not! I'm trapped on an island of homicidal bellboys!

JUNE. Now don't be so frightened. It seems like you don't know how to relate to people.

PUMPHREY. What do you mean?

JUNE. If you feel someone here is upsetting, just shift the focus.

PUMPHREY. Shift the focus?

JUNE. Divert attention. Find something of interest you can point out. Like, (*Pointing to the wall hanging.*) look, there's a bamboo lizard.

PUMPHREY. (*Frightened. Jumping behind her.*) Where?!

JUNE. That wall hanging. You see, I'm trying to show you a way of increasing communication. This is a way of connecting with people.

PUMPHREY. Pointing out bamboo lizards?! Do me a favor, will you? Don't help me anymore with social interaction. I can't take the stress.

JUNE. It's just that you have such a negative attitude. I think it's important for you to confront what's bothering you.

PUMPHREY. Let me explain something. In life, you don't confront what's bothering you, you avoid what's bothering you and then it doesn't bother you.

JUNE. So what are you going to do now?

PUMPHREY. That's what's bothering me. What I was thinking was ... what I was hoping was that for just one night, maybe you could let me stay here.

JUNE. Oh dear, I wouldn't mind, but ...

PUMPHREY. I'll be good and polite. Don't worry that I'll try to, you know ...

JUNE. Well, it's not me. Having talked to you and gotten to know you and everything, I'm sure you're completely trustworthy. Completely!

PUMPHREY. Oh, good, because I was ... (*Pause.*) Could you not say "completely" that way. It hurts my feelings.

JUNE. Really, though, my problem is appearance.

PUMPHREY. Oh, I wouldn't worry about that. You're very attractive.

JUNE. No, I mean, how would it appear to others if you stayed here? Don't forget, I'm now on this island on behalf of the United States Government.

PUMPHREY. Oh, I'm sure the government wouldn't mind. What with one thing and another, they've been so busy lately they might not even notice.

JUNE. It's the officials; Mr. Porter and the general and Mr. Rushmore. Mr. Rushmore, especially, might not approve. He seems like a very moral, upright sort of person.

PUMPHREY. Look, if they come, I'll hide. (*Pause.*) It's just for one night. (*Pause.*) Please!!

JUNE. Well ...

PUMPHREY. Please!!!

JUNE. O.K. But you *promise* you'll hide if those men come?

PUMPHREY. Promise.

(*The TELEPHONE rings. While JUNE is talking, PUMPHREY takes off his jacket and puts it on the bed.*)

JUNE. Hello? Yes. Oh. (*Coldly.*) Hello, Mr. Porter. Yes. Yes, I'm still quite upset. No, don't come up. I have to take a shower. Yes, the suitcase is right here. All right. Goodbye. (*SHE hangs up.*) Honestly! I think they should screen government workers. These two have two so little interest in personal growth aerobic programs.

PUMPHREY. I'm afraid that's true of too many government workers.

JUNE. Oh, it's upsetting. And the way they talked to me and everything. Very, very upsetting. I'm going to take a shower and try to calm down. I won't be very long.

PUMPHREY. O.K. Listen, thanks so much. I really appreciate it. You go do that. I'll just sit here and relax and read my anti-terrorist handbook.

(*JUNE goes into the bathroom. PUMPHREY gets out the handbook and starts reading.*

In the lobby, VICTORIA enters from Upstage. SHE winces when SHE sees KEITH, piña colada in hand, entering from Stage Left. Not yet seen by him, SHE tries to exit. KEITH spots her.)

KEITH. Victoria! What are you doing back here?

VICTORIA. I was afraid I was going to run into you. The plane got cancelled. I'm stuck here for another day. But that doesn't mean I'm going to be in your godawful movie.

KEITH. Don't worry about it. We've gotten a replacement.

VICTORIA. The poor thing. And she's willing to do all the nasty stuff you and Rushmore have cooked up?

KEITH. It's my impression she could cook up even nastier stuff herself.

VICTORIA. Now that's hard to believe. What kind of an actress is she?

KEITH. Actually, her acting background hasn't been explored. (*HE sits on the hassock.*) Mainly we've been impressed with her incredible willingness.

VICTORIA. What do you mean?

KEITH. She's a pro. She's a love professional.

VICTORIA. A pro, huh? Keith, this is totally vulgar. Uch! Next thing you'll tell me is, she comes complete with a parasitic bully who takes all her money.

KEITH. Well, she sort of does.

VICTORIA. What do you mean?

KEITH. There are these two guys, and one in particular seems sort of like her boss, or something.

VICTORIA. You should be ashamed of yourself.

KEITH. Me?

VICTORIA. Yes, you. Ashamed of yourself. She's American?

KEITH. (*Weakly.*) Yes.

VICTORIA. Yuch. Do you know what that's called when an American girl is flown into another country and made to do indecent things?

KEITH. Show business?

VICTORIA. White slavery!

KEITH. Well, not if she agrees to it.

VICTORIA. Keith, for a filthy-minded little twerp, you're sort of innocent.

KEITH. Do I say "thank you" here?

VICTORIA. Sort of unworldly. I mean, look around. People get sucked into sick situations all the time without agreeing to anything.

KEITH. I don't think that ...

VICTORIA. Read the papers! Cult. Mind control. Brainwashing. It's the major theme of this century! It's how the world got to be the way it is! We're talking about history! Didn't you study world history?

KEITH. No. I was absent that week.

VICTORIA. Well, you're still absent! I mean, wake up! Everyone's turning into immoral zombies and you're tagging along!

KEITH. Come on, Victoria, don't get so emotional!

VICTORIA. Emotional!? Don't get so emotional? It's your kind of lazy selfishness that allows the rot to fester and grow!

KEITH. Hey! Why pick on me? I'm not the one living off this girl's ill-gotten gains. Go complain to those men.

VICTORIA. And you think I won't! Let me tell you something: I'm glad my plane was cancelled! I'm going to help that girl pull out of this disgusting situation! Where is she staying?

KEITH. (*Looking away.*) I don't think I should tell you.

VICTORIA. (*Standing next to him.*) Look at me, Keith. Look right at me.

(*Because he's seated, when HE turns to her, he is eye-level with her ample chest. HE is transfixed.*)

VICTORIA. Up, Keith. Look up here.

(*HE looks into her eyes.*)

VICTORIA. *Where is she staying?*
KEITH. Room 203.
VICTORIA. (*Patting him.*) Good boy. Goodbye. (*SHE gets on the elevator.*)
KEITH. Goodbye. Oh boy! I better go tell George!

(*HE tears up the stairs, KNOCKS on Rushmore's door, and is let in just before ELAINE steps off the elevator. ELAINE KNOCK KNOCKS at June's door.*)

PUMPHREY. (*Through the door.*) You're not the porter, are you?
VICTORIA. No.
PUMPHREY. (*Opens door.*) I'm so glad.
VICTORIA. So you're her big, tough friend, huh? (*Marching into the room*) Where is she?
PUMPHREY. In the bathroom.
VICTORIA. Licking her wounds?
PUMPHREY. I guess you could say that.
VICTORIA. I want to tell you something.
PUMPHREY. Yes?
VICTORIA. You make me absolutely sick.
PUMPHREY. Me?
VICTORIA. Totally, thoroughly, disgustingly sick.
PUMPHREY. I know I often don't make a good first impression, but ...
VICTORIA. You are repulsive.
PUMPHREY. Could I get a second opinion on that?
VICTORIA. You think just because she's a woman you can exploit her.
PUMPHREY. Who? June? (*Suddenly thinking she's referring to him staying with June.*) Oh. You mean about

me being *here* ... well, I think "exploit" is a little strong. You see, I was desperate.

VICTORIA. They all are.

PUMPHREY. I have a sort of thing about scary stuff—violence, killing, that sort of thing ...

VICTORIA. You think because I'm a woman you can frighten me, but do you want me to tell you something?

PUMPHREY. (*Unenthusiastically.*) Pretty much.

VICTORIA. You don't scare me at all. You just make me sick.

PUMPHREY. I think you covered that quite well earlier.

VICTORIA. (*Going to the door and opening it.*) It's over. I want you to get out!

PUMPHREY. No, you see, there's some sort of misunderstanding. June said I could stay. (*HE calls toward the bathroom.*) June! June!

VICTORIA. (*Standing in the doorway, pointing to the hall.*) Get out!

PUMPHREY. June!

VICTORIA. Get out!

PUMPHREY. JUNE!

VICTORIA. GET OUT!

PUMPHREY. (*Suddenly inspired, HE points towards the wall handing.*) Oh, my God, look! A bamboo lizard!

(*VICTORIA, startled, jumps back into the hall and PUMPHREY manages to shut the door in her face. HE leans his back into the door.*)

VICTORIA. (*Now stuck out in the hall.*) Open up, creep. Open up! You open that door or things are going to get even worse!

PUMPHREY. I'm not opening it. Go away!

VICTORIA. All right, schmuck, I'm going, but I'll be back. From now on, your kind of scum can't get away with what you do. (*Storms off, going down the elevator and exiting.*)

PUMPHREY. "With what I do?" What's she got against against teaching chemistry?

JUNE. (*Emerging from the bathroom, in a discreet bathrobe.*) I'm done. Oh, I feel so much better. Were you talking to somebody out here?

PUMPHREY. Yes. It was horrible. This awful woman came in and made a big point about how I make her sick.

JUNE. My goodness! You must have misunderstood.

PUMPHREY. No, she couldn't have been more clear about it.

JUNE. But who was she?

PUMPHREY. I've never seen her before. She's a complete stranger.

JUNE. But what was her point about you being sickening?

PUMPHREY. I don't know. She was very ... (*Pause.*) Could you not say that like it's a fact that I'm sickening?

JUNE. I just don't understand. What was she doing in this room?

PUMPHREY. As far as I could tell, her main, central purpose in being here seemed to be ... abuse.

JUNE. You know what? I'll bet she works for the hotel and she was coming to inspect something.

PUMPHREY. Like what?

JUNE. (*Inspired.*) I'll bet she was the hotel bed inspector.

PUMPHREY. June, there is no such occupation as the hotel bed inspector. The job of hotel bed inspector does not exist. That woman was just a free-lance abuser.

JUNE. Nobody goes around being ugly to people for no reason. I think you have been doing negative projection again.

PUMPHREY. I haven't. I've been sticking very closely to my life philosophy: Stay clear of controversy, avoid problems, and don't get involved.

JUNE. Come on. That doesn't sound like a helpful philosophy. I think it's bad to go through life with no commitments. Think how terrible things would be if nobody believed in anything.

PUMPHREY. Terrible? It's beliefs that cause all the trouble. This believer doesn't believe that believer and that believer doesn't believe this believer and then they get in some big war over their beliefs. It's unbelievable.

JUNE. Isn't there anything you'd want to stand up for?

PUMPHREY. (*Sitting down.*) Yes. My right not to have to stand up for anything.

JUNE. You know what I think the problem is?

PUMPHREY. What?

JUNE. That you don't like people.

PUMPHREY. You might be on to something there.

JUNE. And the reason you don't like people is because you don't like yourself.

PUMPHREY. I *do* like myself.

JUNE. If you really did you'd take care of yourself.

PUMPHREY. Who says I don't?

JUNE. Do you? Do you exercise?

PUMPHREY. Sometimes.

JUNE. When?

PUMPHREY. Does running from porters count?

JUNE. I'm going to help you begin a total program of self-improvement.

PUMPHREY. That's very kind of you, but I don't think ...

JUNE. And we're going to start off with a nutritious beverage. (*JUNE goes into the bathroom.*)

PUMPHREY. (*Worried.*) We are? I don't think that's necessary. Let's not. What is it?

(*From inside the bathroom, JUNE can be partially seen mixing the drink.*)

JUNE. It's a drink. A drink I make out of water and dehydrated blue-green algae.

PUMPHREY. Algae?

JUNE. Sure. Blue-green algae.

PUMPHREY. None for me.

JUNE. If you're going to stay here, you have to have some. House rules.

PUMPHREY. No, really. I don't care for any, and I'd hate to waste perfectly good algae.

JUNE. Be a good sport.

PUMPHREY. Also, I promised myself that this year I wouldn't drink anything made from pond scum.

JUNE. (*Coming out of the bathroom with his drink.*) Now don't be a baby. (*SHE hands him the drink.*) Come on, bottoms up. (*Confidentially.*) That's the name of my fitness program.

PUMPHREY. Catchy.

JUNE. Thank you. Now enjoy your drink and I'll go get mine. (*SHE goes back into the bathroom*)

PUMPHREY. O.K. Here goes. (*HE gingerly takes a sip, makes a bitter, cringing face, and then dumps the drink out the window. HE looks out after it, then pulls back inside.*) Mmmm, delicious. But no more for me. I'm full.

JUNE. (*Reentering.*) Did you like it?

PUMPHREY. "Like" isn't the word.

JUNE. It's got a nice texture, doesn't it?

PUMPHREY. Yes, (*Looking to window.*) it goes down very well.

JUNE. Let me show you how to mix it up so that if you get thirsty you can make your own.

PUMPHREY. I may not get that thirsty.

(*THEY go into the bathroom.*
SCOPEC enters the lobby from Upstage, followed by SMITH. Scopec's head and shoulders are covered with the blue-green algae drink. Nothing is said for a moment, and then SMITH begins trying to towel off the mess.)

SMITH. Here you go. We'll dry this off, wipe you all clean. There. Good as new, practically.

SCOPEC. It's sticky. It's sticky and revolting. What is this stuff?

SMITH. (*Sniffing at Scopec's shirt.*) Smells like pond scum.

SCOPEC. Somebody dumped this on me, and I tell you, it was from your exercise woman's room.

SMITH. I don't know, Mr. Scopec, it could have been any room.

SCOPEC. I get hit. I look up and I seen a man ducking back into a window, and I tell you it was *her* window.

SMITH. But that's dumb. Well, it's not dumb. But it's not smart. I guess it could be smart, but, well ... there's no man with June.

SCOPEC. (*HE grabs Smith.*) No man, huh?! What if this girl is not as dumb as she seems, or as you are? What if she's figured this whole stupid thing out and she's fixing to pull out with the cash and she's got some boyfriend to help her? Huh?

SMITH. Well, that's possible, but I ...

SCOPEC. I think that's what's happened, and if I'm right, blood is going to spill. I've had it. You're in danger, that woman is in danger, and if there's a man in there, he is in a lot of danger. Do you remember what happened to Johnny the Finger? (*SCOPEC holds up his pinky.*)

SMITH. Please, Mr. Scopec. I asked you not to bring up Johnny again. (*HE drops the towel on the floor, goes to the elevator, and pushes the button.*)

SCOPEC. Do you remember the—(*SCOPEC pantomimes breaking something and does sound effect.*) and the—(*HE does another violent simulation, and then another. At each jolt, SMITH does horrible wincing movement.*)

SMITH. Yeah, I do.

(*The elevator door opens and the MEN get on.*)

SCOPEC. (*As the door closes.*) And the (*Grunt.*), and the (*Grunt.*) ...

(*The PORTER enters carrying a drink tray. HE sees the towel on the floor and picks it up. HE sniffs it and makes a horrible face. HE takes it over to the window and tosses it out, watching it float down to the rocks below. Then HE exits.*

SCOPEC and SMITH get off the elevator.)

SCOPEC. ... and the (*Grunt..*) and the (*Grunt.*)

SMITH. Right. I remember.

SCOPEC. Now let's go see if she's got company.

SMITH. Good idea. But remember, you're a government official. We don't want her to get suspicious.

SCOPEC. Yeah, yeah.

SMITH. And also, don't forget to apologize.

SCOPEC. Why do *I* need to apologize?

SMITH. We got to keep her happy so she doesn't complain to anybody about us.

SCOPEC. Let's get this over with. (*HE KNOCKS.*)

JUNE. (*From the bathroom.*) Coming! Who is it?

SMITH. It's Mr. Porter and the general.

JUNE. (*Entering from the bathroom and whispering back to Pumphrey.*) Now stay in there and don't come out. They are the unfriendly officials. If they see you, my whole program could be over (*Loudly.*) Coming! (*SHE opens the door slightly.*) Hello. (*SHE suddenly sees Pumphrey's jacket lying on the bed. To Smith and Scopec.*) Oh, sorry. Wait one second. (*SHE closes the door and in a stage whisper says:*) Raymond! Quick! Your jacket! Get your jacket! I'll keep them outside. (*SHE steps into the hall.*) Hello, again. Is everything going O.K.?

(*While June is in the hall, PUMPHREY rushes into the room, slamming the bathroom door behind him. HE runs to the bed, picks up the jacket, and runs back to the bathroom door. It is stuck. HE pulls on it frantically.*)

SMITH. Well, it's going pretty well when you consider all the things that could happen, especially ...

SCOPEC. Drop it, Smith. (*To June.*) We want to talk to you inside.

JUNE. Inside?

SCOPEC. Yeah. Inside your room. Let's go.

JUNE. (*Loudly for Pumphrey's benefit.*) Well, I guess it's all right.

(*As SHE opens the door, PUMPHREY finally manages to pull the bathroom door open, but it's too late for him to do anything but hide behind the now wide open door.*

JUNE assumes he got back into bathroom. SCOPEC rushes Downstage to look under the bed.)

SMITH. Miss Sherwood. My friend here has something to say to you.

JUNE. Yes?

SMITH. General?

SCOPEC. Yeah, well, I ...

SMITH. Come on.

SCOPEC. I ... I ...

JUNE. Yes?

SCOPEC. I am sorry for the rude thing I said to you about shutting your big mouth.

SMITH. And?

SCOPEC. (*Has lifted up the bed and seen there's nothing under it. Loudly.*) And where is the suitcase!? And is there some guy here with you?!

JUNE. Some guy?

SCOPEC. Yeah! I'm asking you, are you hooked up with some guy? Talk!

(*SCOPEC and SMITH have joined June near the bathroom door.*)

JUNE. Do you want me to tell you the truth?

SCOPEC. Yeah.

JUNE. The truth is ... I need to use the bathroom.

SCOPEC. Forget it! Don't go anywhere! Where is the suitcase?!

JUNE. It's over there.

(*SHE points towards the Downstage skirted vanity that the suitcase is under, then SHE quickly steps into the bathroom and shuts the door.*

PUMPHREY is exposed, but SCOPEC and SMITH have quickly moved Downstage looking for the suitcase, and their backs are to him. During the following conversation, HE tiptoes to the lizard wall-hanging on the Upstage wall and manages to at least hide his upper body behind it.

SCOPEC and SMITH are on their hands and knees, looking under the bed.)

SCOPEC. I tell you, Smith, it's not under there. I just looked.

SMITH. Well, it's got to be somewhere.

SCOPEC. I'll tell you where it is. It's in the bathroom. It's in the bathroom with the guy who dumped this stuff on me!

SMITH. It's definitely not under here.

SCOPEC. All right! That's it! She's had it. He's had it! I'm gonna ... (*HE does more noisy simulations of punishments.*) and ... (*Grunt.*)

SMITH. (*Going up and KNOCKING on the bathroom door.*) Miss Sherwood?

SCOPEC. Open up in there!

JUNE. (*Opening the door.*) Yes?

SMITH. We'd like to join you in there if you don't mind.

JUNE. Well, I ...

SCOPEC. Yeah. We want to search the bathroom.

JUNE. But why?

SCOPEC. Why? 'Cause we enjoy searching bathrooms.

JUNE. O.K.

(*ALL THREE go into the bathroom.*

The PORTER enters the lobby, whistling an island tune. HE starts up the stairs. PUMPHREY tiptoes out from behind the wall-hanging and goes to the door. HE opens it, steps out, and runs to the stairwell, but suddenly halts when HE hears the PORTER's whistle ascending towards him. Panicked, HE rushes back to June's door. The Porter's whistle is getting closer. PUMPHREY is forced back into June's room. HE shuts the door just as the PORTER rounds the corner to the hall. The PORTER gets to the door and knocks: KNOCK KNOCK.)

SMITH. (*Still in the bathroom.*) I'll get it. I'll get it. Coming.

(*PUMPHREY, trapped, dives under the bed.*)

SMITH. (*Going to the door and opening it.*) You!!!

PORTER. You!!! I come back later!!

(*The PORTER retreats to the stairwell and tears down it. SMITH follows, yelling.*)

SMITH. Give me back my wallet! Give me back the gun! Come back here now! Stop! Stop right now! (*Etc.*)

(*The PORTER runs across the lobby and exits, with a yelling SMITH close on his heels.*)

JUNE. (*Entering from the bathroom; in a stage whisper.*) Raymond. Are you here?

PUMPHREY. (*Sticking his head out.*) I'm under the bed.

JUNE. Oh, my goodness! Where's Mr. Porter?

PUMPHREY. Porter went off with the porter. But listen, these guys are dangerous. I don't think they're in the foreign service. I think ...

SCOPEC. (*Reentering from the bathroom.*) What's going on? Who are you talking to? (*Bending over and seeing Pumphrey.*) You! Get out here! Come on! Now!

PUMPHREY. (*Crawling out.*) Well, hello. Isn't this a ...

SCOPEC. What do you think you're doing? Who are you!?

PUMPHREY. Me?! Who am I?! Oh, well, I'm ... ah ... I'm ah ... (*Suddenly inspired.*) I'm the Hotel Bed Inspector!

SCOPEC. The what?

PUMPHREY. The Hotel Bed Inspector. Yup. (*HE kicks the side of the bed.*) Everything seems to be working well now with this unit, but if it acts up again, just give me a call.

SCOPEC. Hotel Bed Inspector?

PUMPHREY. Oh yes. We try to stay on top of the whole sleeping equipment situation here at the hotel. Try to—

(*SCOPEC is getting closer. To escape, PUMPHREY jumps up on the bed.*)

PUMPHREY. —safety test each unit thoroughly—(*HE is jumping up and down on the bed, leaping away from Scopec.*)—before and during each visitor's stay, and I'm happy to report that everything seems to be functioning well, and so I guess I'll leave. (*HE jumps off the bed and heads for the door.*)

SCOPEC. Wait. I'm not through with you! (*HE grabs PUMPHREY and backs him into a corner by the bed.*)

PUMPHREY. Oh yes. Of course. (*HE gets on the bed and crawls across it towards June.*) Excuse me. How forgetful. You're so right. I haven't given you the bed inspection clearance release form. (*HE gets to June and gives her a piece of paper.*) As I said, ma'am, there should be any more trouble, but this warranty protects you against unexpected mattress malfunction.

(*SCOPEC tries to catch him.*)

PUMPHREY. No. Sorry. One form to a customer. (*To escape Scopec, HE once again jumps on the bed.*) Oops, got to run.

(*With a mighty leap, HE jumps to the door, bursts through it, and tears down the stairs.*
SCOPEC runs out after him, but then rushes back into June's room.)

SCOPEC. What is this?! Has he set something up with the suitcase?! Where *is* the suitcase?!

JUNE. I will not stand for you to harass me anymore about that suitcase!

SCOPEC. Where is it?!

JUNE. (*SHE folds her arms and turns her back to him.*) I won't discuss it.

SCOPEC. Lady, I'm through with you messing with me. Did he stash it somewhere? Is that where he went?!

(*JUNE ignores him.*)

SCOPEC. Is it downstairs?! (*HE starts towards the door.*) You're getting yourself into a lot of trouble. (*HE runs out the door, rushes to the elevator, pushes the button, and gets on.*)

(*PUMPHREY arrives in the lobby and is about to flee out the Upstage entrance when HE hears:*)

SMITH. (*Offstage.*) Stop! You! Stop! Come back here! Give those back!

(*PUMPHREY dives behind the scuba stand. The PORTER rushes Onstage furtively, carrying something. HE exits Stage Left, and right afterwards, SMITH runs Onstage. Above the waist HE is wearing his jacket, black shirt and white tie. Below; boxer shorts.*)

SMITH. Come back here! Give those back! Do you hear me! Give those ...

SCOPEC. (*Getting off the elevator.*) SMITH!

(*SMITH freezes.*)

SCOPEC. Have you seen him? Have you seen the guy?

SMITH. What guy?

SCOPEC. (*Rapidly.*) I was right. She had someone with her. There was a guy up there. I think he's set up something. I think he's got the suitcase. He's down here somewhere. I'm going to find him. I'm gonna kill him. That's it! Forget it. He's gonna ... (*Pause.*) Where are your pants?

SMITH. Um ... I got hot.

SCOPEC. I'm never working with you again. Go put your pants on and cover the hotel entrance. I'll check out the back.

(*SMITH exits Stage Right, SCOPEC exits Upstage. PUMPHREY's head rises up from the scuba stand. HE tiptoes gingerly towards the Stage Left door, but just as HE gets there HE hears:*)

SEÑORA. (*Offstage.*) Oh yes. I am so honored to have you as a guest in this hotel.

(*PUMPHREY rushes back to behind the scuba stand. SEÑORA enters.*)

SEÑORA. Raoul! (*SHE crosses quickly to the Upstage door.*) Raoul! Raoul! (*SHE exits.*)

(*PUMPHREY again tiptoes to the Stage Left doorway. This time HE hears:*)

VICTORIA. (*Offstage.*) Señora! Señora Valdez!

(*PUMPHREY rushes back to the stand and just gets behind it as VICTORIA enters.*)

VICTORIA. (*Calling out.*) Señora! Señora!

SEÑORA. (*Entering from Upstage.*) Yes, my dear?

(*THEY meet at the scuba stand.*)

VICTORIA. I just think you should know that there is man here who is ... well, he's up to no good.

(*THEY are facing Downstage and can't see that PUMPHREY is now crawling to the elevator.*)

SEÑORA. Is he tall with a bow tie?

VICTORIA. Yes. That's him. You know about him?

SEÑORA. Oh, yes. From the moment I saw him. Look I have his card.

VICTORIA. Oh, great! They're using business cards now.

SEÑORA. But don't worry! He is not supposed to be here. I have people searching all over for him. We will find him.

(*PUMPHREY, from his crawl position, tries to reach the button, but is afraid HE is about to be seen. HE quickly crawls back to the scuba stand.*)

VICTORIA. There are a few others I'm not happy about, but I'm going to handle them myself.

SEÑORA. Good. Now come with me and we will search by the cliff.

(*THEY exit Upstage.*

PUMPHREY makes another attempt to exit Stage Left and is almost out the door when HE sees something Offstage. HE dashes back to the stand. Just as HE gets out of sight, the PORTER, RUSHMORE, and JUNE enter from respectively, the Upstage lobby entrance, room 201, and June's bathroom door. In unison, but unaware of each other, THEY take a few steps forward, and adjust their belts. JUNE: the belt on her shift, which SHE has put back on; RUSHMORE: the belt to his pants which he wants to look tidy for his visit to June; and the PORTER: the belt to Smith's pants which he has so recently acquired.

That done, THEY go about their business. The PORTER exits Stage Left, JUNE gets the suitcase and puts it on the bed, and RUSHMORE goes up to the door and KNOCKS.)

RUSHMORE. (*KNOCK KNOCK*) June. June.

JUNE. (*Coming out of the bathroom.*) Hello. Who is it?

RUSHMORE. George Rushmore.

JUNE. (*SHE opens the door.*) Oh, hello. Come on in. Did you get your call?

RUSHMORE. Call? What call? Oh yes. A very important call. A call from the coast.

JUNE. I guess on an island this small, any call is a call from the coast.

RUSHMORE. Right. But it's probably just as well we were interrupted, because we were getting off to a problematic start with all that leaping and jumping. Let's go rethink that. (*Behind his back HE eases June's door shut and suggestively says:*) It wasn't really what I had in mind.

JUNE. You know, I think you're right. (*SHE crosses to the bed and sits down.*) What I was doing wasn't ...

RUSHMORE. (*Joining her on the bed.*) Intimate enough?

JUNE. That's a good way to put it. (*SHE looks into the distance.*) We want to begin with something quieter, more ... yes, more intimate.

(*RUSHMORE's arms are about to encircle the unsuspecting June when SHE suddenly snaps her fingers, stands up, and announces.*)

JUNE. Leg lifts!

RUSHMORE. (*He encircles air and tips over.*) Leg lifts?

JUNE. Leg lifts. Let me show you. Let's clear this area here so I can spread out.

RUSHMORE. That sounds more like it.

JUNE. (*SHE starts to lift the small chair and then lets out a sob.*) I'm sorry, Mr. Rushmore, I have to speak out. I can't concentrate on this. It's too hard.

RUSHMORE. Well, maybe if I took an end.

JUNE. No. It's not the furniture, it's your associates.

RUSHMORE. My associates?

JUNE. (*Speaking very rapidly; close to tears.*) Yes. They were just here and one of them said earlier he wanted to shut my mouth and then just now he was being very suspicious about a chemistry professor and all either of them talk about is this suitcase, (*SHE is getting weepier.*) and I know it's not my suitcase, but they were so unfriendly that I ...

RUSHMORE. Excuse me. My associates? Do you mean Keith?

JUNE. No, not Keith. Mr. Porter and the general. They *were* from Cleveland and then they changed their minds. I'm sorry to be telling on them, but when I was told I was going to be setting up an aerobics program here on Santa Pequeña ...

RUSHMORE. I'm a little confused.

JUNE. Well, as you know, Mr. Porter and the general learned that by mistake I had their suitcase and that turned out to be a good thing because then they thought of offering me this cultural exchange opportunity.

RUSHMORE. And this is the suitcase?

JUNE. Yes, that's the one. I'm sure you know all about it.

RUSHMORE. What's in it?

JUNE. I thought you would know, because I don't know.

RUSHMORE. Let's take a look.

(*HE opens the suitcase and gasps at its contents. JUNE is across the room and can't see the money.*)

JUNE. What's in it?

RUSHMORE. (*Reverently.*) Lettuce!

JUNE. (*Approaching Rushmore.*) Isn't it getting droopy?

RUSHMORE. (*Slams the suitcase shut before June can see it. Now in a distracted voice ...*) Figure of speech. Now hold on for one second. I need to think a little bit ...

(*Pause.*) Let's confirm, ah, what I already know ... or better still, let's pretend I don't know anything—for confirmation purposes. You are here because ...

JUNE. Because of the cultural exchange program.

RUSHMORE. Because of the cultural exchange program, right, and you are ..

JUNE. June Sherwood, aerobic instructor, who's developed my own special system of exercise called "Bottoms Up" that tones the whole person all at once.

RUSHMORE. O.K. You got this suitcase by mistake from two men who say they are the government and I am also with the government.

(*VICTORIA enters the lobby and gets on the elevator.*)

RUSHMORE. All right. Now this is just a question I have to ask. It is routine. Do you do nude scenes?

JUNE. Mr. Rushmore!

RUSHMORE. Sorry, I hate to ask that, but ... What can I do? It's government policy. We need to know who we're dealing with.

JUNE. But nude scenes?

(*VICTORIA gets off the elevator.*)

RUSHMORE. You'd be surprised at the sorts of people the government gets these days. It has become a very troubling problem.

JUNE. What has?

RUSHMORE. Federal nudity. The State Department office that I work in here has been plagued by ...

VICTORIA. (*KNOCK KNOCK.*) Open up in there!

JUNE. Oh, dear, Mr. Rushmore, ... I forgot to tell you ... there seems to be a woman ...

RUSHMORE. What woman? (*HE opens the door.*)

VICTORIA. (*Entering. To Rushmore.*) You are disgusting!

JUNE. I think this woman.

RUSHMORE. Victoria, I'm so glad to see you.

VICTORIA. A likely story. (*To June.*) And you're the hired body?

JUNE. Well, I do teach, ah ... the hired body?

VICTORIA. Oh, you poor, pathetic thing. Don't worry, I'm not going to let it happen.

RUSHMORE. That's right. It's not going to happen. Victoria—(*Aside to June.*) She works with me at the office. (*To Victoria.*) Victoria, there's been a little confusion here, and June won't be doing what I *originally* had planned for her ...

JUNE. I won't ? But that's what I was looking forward to.

VICTORIA. Yuch.

RUSHMORE. No, don't worry. I have other plans for you and the suitcase. Ah, Victoria, if you would just come with me ... (*HE tries to usher Victoria towards the door.*) Victoria, if you wouldn't mind ...

VICTORIA. Get your hands off me.

RUSHMORE. Come on now.

VICTORIA. Don't touch me, you hideous, slimy manipulator.

JUNE. What did she call you?

RUSHMORE. Ah, don't worry, that's my nickname down at the office.

JUNE. Hideous, slimy manipulator?

RUSHMORE. It's a long nickname. (*HE is busily trying to keep June and Victoria away from each other.*)

VICTORIA. What office?

RUSHMORE. Oh, don't worry. Ah, look, Victoria, come with me. I've got to talk with you. Let me just ...

VICTORIA. About what? What creepy movie deal is he sucking you into?

JUNE. Movie deal?

RUSHMORE. Victoria, I've got to talk to you. Please step into the hall.

JUNE. What movie deal?

VICTORIA. Hasn't he asked you to prance around naked?

JUNE. What?

RUSHMORE. Victoria, please. (*To June, trying to get her out of Victoria's hearing range.*) I'm awfully sorry about her. She's always talking about prancing around naked. We've had to have several sessions with the staff psychiatrist.

VICTORIA. Hasn't he tried to take your clothes off?

RUSHMORE. Victoria, please. Attend a few more sessions.

JUNE. She works for you?

RUSHMORE. We're hiring all types these days.

VICTORIA. Mainly naked types!

RUSHMORE. There she goes again.

JUNE. I don't understand.

RUSHMORE. No one does. We don't yet know what causes Nudity Obsession. Or as doctors call it: skinnydipsodemia.

VICTORIA. What are you driveling on about?

RUSHMORE. I'll explain in a second. Victoria, if you'll step into the hall with me, I have to talk to you. (*To June.*) Government business.

VICTORIA. What government?

JUNE. What about my agenda?

RUSHMORE. That's postponed for the moment.

JUNE. Oh, no!

VICTORIA. Good.

RUSHMORE. It'll be rescheduled very soon. (*HE picks up the suitcase.*) For now, I'll just take the suitcase here, and Victoria and I ...

JUNE. (*Grabbing it away from him.*) No, no, no! You can't have the suitcase! I'm tired of everybody all excited about this suitcase and nobody being interested in what I'm here for!

RUSHMORE. I *am* interested. Very interested, but right now I've got to talk to Victoria, and I, uh ... need to take the suitcase.

JUNE. No! I won't let you. Just leave.

RUSHMORE. But what about the, ah, plans? What about ... you know ... (*HE does obscene-looking aerobics movement.*) Aren't you going to do that?

VICTORIA. (*To Rushmore.*) You sex addict!

RUSHMORE. (*To June.*) Don't mind her. She's really made a lot of progress. (*Reaching for the suitcase.*) So let me just grab this and ...

JUNE. No! (*SHE starts crying.*) I'm feeling very harassed.

VICTORIA. (*Putting her arm around her.*) Now, now. Don't worry. It's O.K. Everything's going to be all right.

JUNE. I know. I know. I *will* do my program. I'm sure of it, but right now I've got to be by myself. I think I'll take a shower.

RUSHMORE. Wonderful idea. Do that. We'll leave. Suitcase?

JUNE. No!

VICTORIA. You're all right?

JUNE. Yes, just leave.

RUSHMORE. (*Timidly going up to her one more time.*) Suitcase?

JUNE. (*Full volume.*) Get out!

(This blast sends him flying to the door. RUSHMORE and VICTORIA step into the hall. JUNE shuts the door behind them and goes into the bathroom.)

RUSHMORE. God, Victoria, you may have ruined everything. What were you trying to do?

VICTORIA. That's easy, I was trying to ruin everything. What creepy, nasty activity are you up to?

RUSHMORE. I can't tell you right now, but it's not creepy and nasty. You've got to believe me!

VICTORIA. I don't believe you.

RUSHMORE. Look, I can explain everything. I've just got to talk to Keith for a second. Why don't you go down to the lobby and I'll meet you there in a few minutes. (*HE pushes the elevator button.*) Then I'll explain the whole thing.

VICTORIA. All right, but this sure smells like another of your yucky projects.

RUSHMORE. Victoria, trust me.

VICTORIA. Please, I just ate.(*The elevator door opens.*)

RUSHMORE. See you in a few minutes.

VICTORIA. Remember, if this has anything to do with coconut oil, you're dead. (*SHE is on the elevator and the doors close.*)

RUSHMORE. (*KNOCKING on his door.*) Keith, open up! Keith! Keith! Come out here. Quick!

(KEITH steps into the hall.)

RUSHMORE. You won't believe this. Guess what?

KEITH. What?

RUSHMORE. I have just had the most amazing thing happen with June.

KEITH. Great. Did you get any of it on film?

RUSHMORE. No, listen, June isn't in the love business. She's some sort of exercise person.

KEITH. Really? What's she doing here?

RUSHMORE. As far as I can tell, she's being duped into a money laundry scheme. She's got a suitcase full of money. Full of it. Jammed with it. Cash! Cash! Cash!

KEITH. Cash?

RUSHMORE. Cash! And, Keith, I had the suitcase in my hand, but Victoria betrayed me.

KEITH. You were going to just take the money?

RUSHMORE. Of course! It's illegal money, dirty money. It's up for grabs. That money is basically mine! Mine! Mine!

KEITH. Except for one thing.

RUSHMORE. What?

KEITH. It's not yours.

RUSHMORE. Don't quibble.

KEITH. But it's not. June's got it.

RUSHMORE. It's mine ... Virtually. Almost ... I've got to get it. Then I can use that money to ... to make more money. Get investors involved. I'll be rich. Rich at last. At last I can make the movies I want to make. No more cheap little productions with unknown naked actresses. With money, I can do big Hollywood productions with famous naked actresses.

KEITH. So are you just going to ask June for the cash?

RUSHMORE. No, right now she's mad at me. I've got to think of some other approach. And I've got to move fast on this thing.

KEITH. It's too bad Victoria doesn't like you.

RUSHMORE. Yeah, well, some do some don't.

KEITH. Most don't. Is June mad at Victoria too?

RUSHMORE. No. It's me they all dislike. June and Victoria were acting very simpatico. They were ... (*Snapping fingers.*) Hold it!

KEITH. What?

RUSHMORE. That's the solution. Victoria. I'll use Victoria. (*HE pushes the elevator button.*)

KEITH. I don't know if Victoria is very usable.

RUSHMORE. For George Rushmore everyone is usable. (*The elevator door opens.*) Here, come on, Keith, I have a plan.

(*THEY get on the elevator.*
PUMPHREY again rises up from the scuba stand, now wearing face mask, snorkel tube, flippers, grass skirt and any other tropical artifact that can be found. As HE heads for the Stage Left exit, VICTORIA enters.)

VICTORIA. (*Not recognizing him.*) Good afternoon.

(*PUMPHREY makes a muffled snorkel noise through his tube and then exits. VICTORIA looks on after him suspiciously.*
RUSHMORE and KEITH get off the elevator. RUSHMORE has assumed a deeply tragic demeanor.)

KEITH. (*Patting Rushmore on the shoulder.*) It's O.K., George. It's O.K.

RUSHMORE. I'm so ashamed! (*HE makes himself break free of Keith and starts walking, distractedly, Downstage.*)

KEITH. Now come on. Come on. It's not your fault.

VICTORIA. All right, Rushmore. What was going on up there?

(*Too grief-stricken to notice her, HE walks past.*)

VICTORIA. Rushmore!

RUSHMORE. (*Still distracted.*) Oh. Hello, Victoria. How are you?

VICTORIA. Don't worry about how I am. Just tell me what was happening with that girl up there.

RUSHMORE. Tell you?

VICTORIA. Yes. You said you'd tell me.

RUSHMORE. Oh, God! I wish I could I wish ... (*HE lets out a sob.*)

VICTORIA. Will you explain what the problem is. Why did you want that suitcase?

(*Unable to hold back any longer, RUSHMORE blubbers tragically and has to be comforted by KEITH.*)

KEITH. (*To Victoria.*) The word "suitcase" seems to set him off.

VICTORIA. (*A little more gently.*) Now settle down. Stop crying and tell me what's gotten you so upset.

RUSHMORE. Do I have to?

VICTORIA. Yes.

(*For the rest of the scene, RUSHMORE is weeping as HE talks.*)

RUSHMORE. That girl. That girl in that room is not what she seems. (*HE is choking out these words.*) I don't know if you met the men she's with ...

VICTORIA. I met one of them and he was pretty much a stomach-turning parasite.

RUSHMORE. Oh, how perceptive—that's exactly what he is. Believe me, I know the type.

VICTORIA. Rushmore, you *are* the type.

RUSHMORE. I understand why you'd say that.

VICTORIA. But what about the suitcase?

RUSHMORE. (*A loud sob.*) That girl is part of an international spy ring. (*HE sits down on the hassock.*)

VICTORIA. Come on.

RUSHMORE. An international ring of mercenary spies who will cheerfully sell out the land of their birth for money.

VICTORIA. They sound like your kind of guys.

RUSHMORE. June has smuggled out classified documents and she's in the middle of a deal to sell them to you-know-who.

VICTORIA. Who?

RUSHMORE. You know, ah ... the enemy.

VICTORIA. Who *is* the enemy these days?

RUSHMORE. Ah ... (*Suddenly inspired.*) Who isn't?

VICTORIA. And where did she get these documents?

RUSHMORE. Oh, it's an all too familiar story. She hung out at military bases. Got friendly with low-level personnel—a couple of well-situated privates—and under the spell of those men I mentioned, she got these privates to hand over vital information. They call it ... Operation ... (*The floodgates open.*) Bottoms Up!!! (*Blurting these last two words out is so tragic HE has to wrap himself around Keith's waist and sob some more.*)

VICTORIA. Even if this were true ...

RUSHMORE. It's true!

VICTORIA. Even if it were, why are you so upset? Just call the authorities.

RUSHMORE. (*Rising in alarm.*) I can't do that!

VICTORIA. Why not?

RUSHMORE. Because I discovered something else while I was up there. Something so shattering that ... (*Sobbing on Keith's shoulder again.*)

KEITH. (*Patting him.*) There, there.

VICTORIA. What did he discover?

RUSHMORE. While I was up, there, I discovered that that girl is ... (*Emotionally.*) my daughter!

VICTORIA. Your daughter?!

RUSHMORE. My daughter.

KEITH. His daughter.

RUSHMORE. I found out that she's the little girl I left behind years ago. I feel responsible for what she's become. Suddenly, I saw what she was doing and what I had to do.

VICTORIA. And what was that?

RUSHMORE. Get that suitcase. Suddenly I saw the squalor of my life and the chance I was being given to change it. And I almost was able to do it, to take the suitcase, when you came in. (*Emotionally.*) My once chance to help my daughter and my country is thwarted.

VICTORIA. Oh, come on now, you'll have another chance.

RUSHMORE. No. Now she distrusts me. It's over. (*HE weeps on Keith's shoulder.*)

VICTORIA. Well, maybe I could talk to her.

RUSHMORE. (*His head instantly popping up.*) What a wonderful idea.

VICTORIA. I'll call her up from the lobby phone, get her to come down here—neutral territory—and maybe we can straighten this out.

RUSHMORE. (*HE collapses into her arms.*) Oh, God! Victoria! Thank you! Thank you! Thank you! And tell her to bring the suitcase. We'll leave you here. Good luck.

(*RUSHMORE and KEITH start leaving.*)

RUSHMORE. And thank you.

KEITH. Yes, and thank you.

RUSHMORE. And suitcase.

KEITH. And suitcase.

(*THEY exit. VICTORIA goes to the Lobby phone, but just after SHE picks it up, PUMPHREY enters, walking backwards in a frightened way. HE doesn't see her.*)

VICTORIA. So there you are!

(*PUMPHREY jumps in alarm.*)

VICTORIA. It turns out you're even worse than I thought.

PUMPHREY. I am? Oh, God!

VICTORIA. I want to talk to you.

PUMPHREY. I can't talk. I've got to go. (*HE runs off.*)

VICTORIA. Wait a second. I've got something to say to you. (*SHE follows him Offstage.*)

(*JUNE comes out of the bathroom with a handful of celery sticks. SHE is eating one of them.*

PUMPHREY tears into the lobby from the Upstage entrance, looking terrified. HE jumps behind the hassock just as SCOPEC and SMITH enter, running. SMITH is still wearing his jacket and tie and has put on a flashy, tropical pair of Bermuda shorts.)

SCOPEC. That was him! That was the guy! He's gonna die! And I'm gonna kill him!

SMITH. He definitely came this way. And he definitely went out there, probably.

(*SCOPEC and SMITH exit. PUMPHREY rises and quickly goes to the stairwell. HE rushes up the stairs, arriving, out of breath, at June's door.*)

PUMPHREY. Help! Oh, God! June, please open up! June! June!

JUNE. Is that you, Raymond?

PUMPHREY. Just barely. Open up!

(*JUNE opens the door and HE enters.*)

JUNE. What's the matter? Where did you go?

PUMPHREY. June, they're after me!

JUNE. Who?

PUMPHREY. Everybody!

JUNE. Why?

PUMPHREY. In this place who needs a reason!

JUNE. Well, they must have said something?

PUMPHREY. Yes, your friend, the government aerobics coordinator, said that I was going to die! And he was going to kill me!

JUNE. You must have misunderstood. Did you ask him if that's what he really meant?

PUMPHREY. You don't ask people to clarify death threats!

JUNE. It couldn't have been a death threat.

PUMPHREY. It was a death threat! A death threat! A death threat!

JUNE. You're hysterical. Now calm down. Take a deep breath. Exhale. Inhale. Exhale. Inhale. Good. Now, crouch position.

(*PUMPHREY is following along.*)

JUNE. Down. Up. Down ...

PUMPHREY. (*Out of breath and patience.*) Will you stop! I need help saving my life, not thigh-trimming! Help! Help! Hel ...

JUNE. (*Stops his cries by pushing a celery stick in his mouth.*) Now just settle down.

PUMPHREY. (*Pulling the stalk out.*) How can you expect me to settle down?

JUNE. I want you to sit. (*SHE seats him on the bed and sits down beside him.*) O.K.? Now listen. You're being negative.

PUMPHREY. I'm not being nega ...

JUNE. (*Pushing the stalk back in his mouth.*) Yes you are. You've got to be more open to the positive. Less rigid. More intuitive. Now *I'm* not very happy with the attitude of some of these government people, but ...

PUMPHREY. (*Removing the stalk.*) Attitude? June! They want to kill me. To kill me! Help! Help! Help! Hel ...

(*JUNE leans over and kisses him.*)

PUMPHREY. (*Weakly.*) Help.

JUNE. Now just settle down.

PUMPHREY. Why did you do that?

JUNE. I don't know. You're so upset. I suddenly felt that's what I should do.

PUMPHREY. (*Pause.*) Do you want to do it again?

(*THEY kiss.*)

JUNE. (*Rising.*) Now don't get any ideas. I'm not a forward person. I just wanted to help you. Maybe you've stirred up some sort of maternal feeling.

PUMPHREY. Come on. I don't stir up maternal feeling in my *mother*.

(*VICTORIA enters the lobby, picks up the phone and dials.*)

JUNE. I kissed you 'cause I wanted to calm you down.

PUMPHREY. (*Joining her.*) It worked. I'm much calmer. (*Putting his arms around her.*) In fact, I feel like ...

(*The PHONE rings.*)

JUNE. (*Seating him back on the bed.*) Now just sit there quietly. (*SHE picks up the phone.*) Hello.

VICTORIA. June? June? Is that you?

JUNE. Yes, this is me. Who's this?

VICTORIA. It's Victoria. We just met a little bit ago.

JUNE. Oh, yes.

VICTORIA. June, are you alone?

JUNE. Well, I'm not sure I should ...

VICTORIA. Is there someone there with you?

JUNE. O.K. Yes, there is.

VICTORIA. All right, listen. Is it the person, the man, I had the encounter with when I first came up to your room?

JUNE. Well, I don't know ...

(*PUMPHREY is having trouble getting comfortable.*)

VICTORIA. June, I want to help you, but I can't if you won't cooperate. When I first came up to your room there was a man there.

(*PUMPHREY is shifting around on the bed.*)

VICTORIA. He was tall, with dark hair and a very shifty quality. Is he there with you now?

JUNE. Well, yeah, I guess so.

VICTORIA. June, that man is vermin.
JUNE. No, I think he's from the United States.

(*PUMPHREY starts eating the celery.*)

VICTORIA. June, he's scum. I want you to look at him right now. Are you looking at him?
JUNE. Yes.
VICTORIA. I want you to notice what I noticed about him. Look at his face. Look at his thick, brutish brow and his squinty eyes.

(*PUMPHREY has got some celery caught between his teeth, so his face scrunches up as HE tries to get it out with his tongue.*)

PUMPHREY. (*Stage whisper.*) Celery fibers are stuck.
VICTORIA. June, this man is exploiting you. He's trying to get everything he can out of you.
PUMPHREY. (*Standing up.*) June, can I use your bathroom?

(*JUNE waves him inside.*)

VICTORIA. He's using you. He doesn't care about you, he just wants what you've got.
PUMPHREY. (*Poking his head back into the room.*) Can I use your dental floss?
JUNE. (*SHE nods and waves him back in.*) I think you're wrong about him.
VICTORIA. June, I know what it's like to be under someone's spell. These kind of people know how to create a worldly, cosmopolitan facade that dazzles you and weakens your self-image. I'm sure he's got a very sophisticated approach.

PUMPHREY. (*Poking HIS head back out, the floss dangling from his teeth.*) Now the dental floss is stuck too. (*HIS head goes back into the bathroom.*)

JUNE. I *know* you're wrong about him.

VICTORIA. Look, just give me a chance. I want to talk to you face to face and try to help you with this situation.

JUNE. Well, if you really feel strongly about it.

VICTORIA. I do. And, June, where is your "friend" now?

JUNE. He's in the bathroom.

VICTORIA. Do me this one favor. I want you to leave that room right now. I don't want you to tell him you're going.

JUNE. But I have to make ...

VICTORIA. No. No, June, you don't. Trust me. Hang up the phone and walk out the door.

JUNE. But I ...

VICTORIA. (*Intensely.*) Hang up the phone and walk out the door.

JUNE. O.K.

(*THEY BOTH hang up. JUNE tiptoes out of the room.*)

PUMPHREY. (*Offstage.*) Hey, June. I'm giving your technique a try. I'm taking a shower.

(*JUNE rings for the elevator and when the doors open, gets on. RUSHMORE and KEITH enter the lobby.*)

RUSHMORE. Did you talk to her? Is she coming down?

VICTORIA. Yes. She's coming right now. I think I may be able to help her.

RUSHMORE. Oh, that's wonderful. Oh, I'm so happy. We're going to pick up the pieces of my daughter's life at last and really, my life too, and is she going to bring the suitcase?

VICTORIA. No.

RUSHMORE. No?

KEITH. No?

VICTORIA. No. I thought I'd better take it one thing at a time.

RUSHMORE. And she's coming right away?

VICTORIA. Right away.

RUSHMORE. Victoria, ah ... have a long talk with her and, Keith ...

KEITH. Yes?

RUSHMORE. Come with me.

(THEY start towards the elevator.)

RUSHMORE. No, wait. June's using the elevator. We'll use the stairs.

(THEY rush to the stairway and head up it.)

KEITH. What are we going to do?

RUSHMORE. I've got a plan. There's a ledge out our window. While she's out of her room, we're going to use it.

(THEY dart into Rushmore's room. JUNE steps off the elevator.)

VICTORIA. *(Running up to her and taking her hands.)* June, I'm so glad you're here. This is a start. You've left that man up in your room?

JUNE.Yes, he's still up there, but I think you're misjudging ...

VICTORIA. Don't you understand that he's betraying where he's from?

JUNE. Scranton?

VICTORIA. Ah, yes. Scranton, his country, his life. And you! Your life. What about your life?

JUNE. Excuse me?

VICTORIA. Your life! You haven't made good choices. I mean, you've only got one life.

JUNE. I know. I've seen those beer commercials too.

VICTORIA. Well, it's true. And I don't think you want to throw it away.

JUNE. You're right. I don't. That's why I'm so involved in Bottom's Up.

VICTORIA. Yes, well, I've heard about Operation Bottoms Up. You've got to stop it while you still can.

JUNE. Stop Bottoms Up! Oh, I would never do that.

VICTORIA. But how can you stand to jeopardize your freedom?

JUNE. Oh, no. It makes me more free. It's only a few hours and then I get to do whatever I want.

VICTORIA. You poor thing. And to think I felt sorry for you because of sex and nudity. This is so much worse.

JUNE. Sex and nudity. Don't worry. I understand about your problem with ... exposure.

VICTORIA. *My* problem?

JUNE. I'm sure with the proper help you'll get over it.

VICTORIA. Look, I'm not the one who's going to be publicly exposed.

JUNE. I'm not planning on being publicly exposed.

VICTORIA. Well, you will be. And also, think of those privates. You're also going to expose those privates.

(*Horrified, JUNE covers her lap with her hands, then suddenly points to the lobby's wall-hanging lizard.*)

JUNE. Oh, my God! Look! A bamboo lizard!

(*When VICTORIA turns to look, JUNE darts out the Upstage exit.*)

VICTORIA. (*Rushing after her.*) Wait! Stop! (*SHE exits.*)

(*RUSHMORE comes through June's window and tumbles onto the bed. HE is picking up the suitcase when HE hears:*)

PUMPHREY. (*Offstage.*) You know, June ...

(*As Pumphrey speaks, RUSHMORE, in a panic, jumps back onto the bed and goes under the covers.*)

PUMPHREY. (*Offstage.*) I've made a decision. I've decided I'm beginning to start to agree with you. (*Entering and wandering Downstage as HE talks. He has taken his shower and is dressed as before except he now has on a sleeveless T-shirt. HE is drying his face with a towel and doesn't notice that June is gone.*) I think maybe you're right. I should be more alert to the worthwhile things around me instead of always harping on the negative. Of course, in this place there do seem to be a lot of negative harping opportunities, but maybe there's some subtle communication around here I'm missing. Maybe you have a point. I should be more intuitive. More attuned to the whole range of messages people are sending. I know there's a lot of communication that isn't spoken. Sometimes just a gesture or a body position can ... June? June!? (*HE sees*

Rushmore's lump on the bed.) Oh! Oh, my goodness. You're on the bed. (*Pause.*) You're in the bed! Uh-huh. Well. Is this a message? June? June? (*Pause.*) Joowoon. (*HE sits on the bed and puts his hand on Rushmore.*) June, this is kind of sudden, but ... (*Suddenly making up his mind.*) That's good! Spontaneity! That's what I want more of in my life. I'm going to go with this! I like it! New things! I like surprises!

RUSHMORE. (*Pulling off his covers.*) Surprise!

PUMPHREY. (*In horror.*) Ahhhh!!! (*HE leaps off the bed and backs up to the door.*) Who are you?!

RUSHMORE. Who am I? Who am I? Ah ... I'm, I'm ...

PUMPHREY. I may as well warn you, the bed inspector concept is taken. Tell me who you are.

RUSHMORE. I'm, I'm, I'm ... do you know June very well?

PUMPHREY. No, why?

RUSHMORE. I'm her husband.

PUMPHREY. June, doesn't have a husband.

RUSHMORE. Did she tell you that?

PUMPHREY. No, but ...

RUSHMORE. (*Getting out of bed.*) Well, there you are. And anyhow, enough about me. What are you doing coming out of my wife's bathroom?!

PUMPHREY. Oh, well, I'd gotten some celery stuck between my teeth and then I decided to take a shower.

RUSHMORE. That is an over-reaction to celery. I'm terribly shocked! I think it's an outrage to find a strange man in my room!

(*KEITH tumbles from the window onto the bed.*)

PUMPHREY. Whoops. Here's another outrage.

KEITH. I thought you might need some help in here.

PUMPHREY. If you're her husband, who's this?

RUSHMORE. Why it's ah ... our son. Our little boy.

PUMPHREY. He doesn't seem very little. He's your son? *June's* son!? What's his name?

RUSHMORE. (*Proudly.*) Junior. (*To Keith.*) Come along now, Junior. Don't forget we've got to deliver this suitcase.

(*HE picks up the suitcase and HE and KEITH start to go out the door.*)

PUMPHREY. (*Blocking their path.*) This doesn't seem right. I don't think I should let you take June's suitcase.

KEITH. (*To Rushmore.*) Who is he, dad?

(*THEY edge around Pumphrey and go out the door. PUMPHREY follows.*)

RUSHMORE. (*To Keith.*) This man needed to use Mommy's shower to get some celery out of his teeth.

KEITH. Seems like an over-reaction.

(*ALL THREE start descending the staircase, talking as THEY go.*)

RUSHMORE. You really don't need to see us out, thank you. We're fine.

PUMPHREY. Look, I don't feel right about letting you take June's suitcase.

RUSHMORE. Oh, it's no problem We're happy to do it. Right, Junior?

KEITH. Right, Dad.

PUMPHREY. She just never mentioned having a husband and a son.

RUSHMORE. She probably forgot.

PUMPHREY. Why don't you let me keep the suitcase till she gets back?

RUSHMORE. We wouldn't hear of it.

KEITH. That's right, Pop.

(THEY get to the lobby just as SCOPEC and SMITH enter.)

SCOPEC. Stop! Hold it right there! Give me that suitcase!

RUSHMORE. Oh, sorry! Wrong lobby!

(RUSHMORE, KEITH and PUMPHREY spin around and start tearing back up the stairway. SCOPEC and SMITH take off after them. As THEY are running, JUNE enters the lobby and goes to the elevator. SHE pushes the button, the doors open, and SHE gets on.)

SCOPEC. *(Yelling as HE runs.)* I'm not kidding! Stop or you're dead!! Smith, get out your gun!

SMITH. I've, ah ... lost it.

SCOPEC. You've gone too far, Smith! You're gonna get it! They're gonna get it. Get them! Get these guys! Stop! Give me that suitcase!

SMITH. Give us that suitcase!

(THEY are gaining on Rushmore.)

PUMPHREY. Give them the suitcase!

RUSHMORE. No!! It's mine! It's mine!

(RUSHMORE, KEITH and PUMPHREY arrive at the Upstage end of the hallway. RUSHMORE is grappling with his door. It won't open. HE desperately pushes the elevator button. SCOPEC and SMITH have reached the

top of the stairs. RUSHMORE is cowering in terror. The elevator door opens.)

JUNE. (*From inside.*) Mr. Rushmore!
RUSHMORE. Why, June. Mind if we join you?

(*RUSHMORE dives through the door and is quickly followed by KEITH and PUMPHREY.*)

SCOPEC. (*Rushing down the hall after them.*) Stop! Hold it! Get them, Smith!

(*THEY are able to jump inside the elevator just before the door closes. The elevator floor-indicator goes down as SEÑORA and VICTORIA enter.*)

SEÑORA. So you see, Victoria, respectability is so important to me. I try to maintain a quiet, dignified atmosphere throughout the hotel.

(*The elevator doors open, revealing a snarl of angry bodies. EVERYBODY clawing and yelling, "That's my suitcase!" "Give that back!" "Who are you!" "You're in trouble!" and so on.*
PUMPHREY comes crawling out of this mess, lugging the suitcase with him.)

SEÑORA. You!
VICTORIA. You!
PUMPHREY. Me?!
SEÑORA. You have gone too far this time! You are in a great deal of trouble!

(*MORE BODIES spill out of the elevator.*)

RUSHMORE. Quick! Give me the suitcase!
KEITH. Quick! Toss it to me!

(*PUMPHREY, clutching the suitcase, is darting around the lobby like a kickoff receiver, his pursuers yelling at him in overlapping abuse that gets louder and louder.*)

SCOPEC. Hey, you! You're though, buddy!
SMITH. Come on now, give me the suitcase.
SEÑORA. Now you would steal suitcases!
JUNE. Raymond, what's going on?
SCOPEC. You better stop!!
VICTORIA. Stop right where you are!!
RUSHMORE. Quick, Keith, I've almost got it.
SMITH. You better give it to me!!

(*ETC.*)

PUMPHREY. (*HE has reached the lobby window and in a burst of righteous anger yells at full volume ...*) STOP!!

(*This freezes the GROUP which has gathered Downstage. JUNE is standing on the hassock.*)

PUMPHREY. (*With authority.*) I am through with being chased and pushed around! I am taking a stand! I'm not giving this suitcase back until I find out whose it is!!

SCOPEC. (*Approaching Pumphrey.*) Give me that thing!

PUMPHREY. No!! (*HE holds up the suitcase as if he's about to throw it out the window.*) One step closer and this baby goes out the window!! Now who does this belong to??

SCOPEC. It's mine.

KEITH. (*Pointing to Rushmore.*) It's his.

RUSHMORE. It's mine.

SMITH. (*Pointing to Scopec.*) It's his.

JUNE. It belongs to the United States Government.

PUMPHREY. Is that right?

SMITH. Well, not technically speaking. Technically speaking, (*Pointing at Scopec.*) it's his.

PUMPHREY. Are you government officials?

(*SCOPEC is about to assent to that when ...*)

SMITH. Not really.

(*A scowl from SCOPEC.*)

PUMPHREY. (*Pointing to Rushmore.*) Do *you* work for the U.S. Government?

RUSHMORE. (*Modestly.*) Well, I actually have ...

VICTORIA. Who? Rushmore? He's probably *wanted* by the U.S. Government.

RUSHMORE. Victoria ...

VICTORIA. Admit it, Rushmore. Your story about spies was a big fake!

RUSHMORE. Oh, I suppose in a certain sense ...

VICTORIA. This whole thing stinks! It stinks of fraud and exploitation and you know what else it stinks of?

KEITH. (*Sniffing Scopec.*) Pond scum?

VICTORIA. Greed!!

JUNE. Does this mean I'm not going to conduct my classes?

PUMPHREY. It looks like Bottoms Up is down.

SCOPEC. Look, that's my money and it's true, we were a little deceptive to her so she would give it back to us, but ...

JUNE. A little? I've been made a fool of! (*SHE is emotional.*) There's no government program! It's all a fake! My dreams are kerpluee! It's hopeless! I should have stayed in Toledo!! (*SHE sits down on the hassock and weeps.*)

SMITH. (*Nudging Scopec.*) Say it to her.

SCOPEC. (*Going over to June.*) All right, all right. We're ah ... sorry. Very sorry. (*Rushing back to Pumphrey.*) Now give me back the suitcase!

PUMPHREY. No!

SCOPEC. No?!

PUMPHREY. No, you told her she could conduct an aerobics class, and that's just what she's going to do.. Right now! Everybody! Come on! Get in formation.

(*NOBODY moves.*)

PUMPHREY. Or I'm feeding this to the seagulls.

SCOPEC. No way!

PUMPHREY. I'm not kidding. There's a new Raymond Pumphrey on this island and he's mad! And he's ready to hurt suitcases! June! Do it!!

JUNE. I just don't feel ...

PUMPHREY. Let's go!!

JUNE. (*With a sudden resolve SHE gets up and addresses the group.*) O.K., everybody. O.K. Back up and get in two lines. I'll turn on the radio.

(*The GROUP reluctantly assembles as JUNE puts on the MUSIC.*)

JUNE. Good. Now I want you, in a relaxed way, to get into a jumping rhythm. Come on now. Loosen up.

(*The GROUP halfheartedly mimics her movements.*)

PUMPHREY. Let's go, everybody! Look lively!

(*THEY get a little more animated.*)

JUNE. To the side now. One, two, three, push. One, two, three, push. Now the other side. One, two ... (*JUNE continues yelling out instructions and the dance becomes two coordinated chorus lines of aerobic movement.*) Come on, Raymond, join in.

PUMPHREY. Me? Oh, no.

JUNE. Come on. This is for everyone.

PUMPHREY. Oh ... well ... all right. (*HE puts the suitcase down, gets into the formation and is soon as animated as EVERYBODY ELSE.*)

JUNE. ... now the other way. Forward, two, three, kick. Back, two, three, kick. Forward, two ... (*Etc.*)

(*The PORTER enters, unnoticed by the EXERCISERS. HE too is dancing happily to the rhythm. Suddenly HE spots the unattended suitcase and his face broadens into a delighted grin.*)

JUNE. ... now turn around, two, three, kick. Again, two. three ...

(*Now that the GROUP is facing Upstage, the PORTER goes and picks up the suitcase. HE is sneaking out the exit just as JUNE is getting EVERYONE to bend over with ...*)

JUNE. ... O.K., now, bottoms up!

CURTAIN

COSTUME PLOT

JUNE

Act I: Makes her first entrance carrying a snazzy, mod athletic bag. A camera hangs from a strap around her neck. She is wearing an easy-fitting dress, pretty but unsophisticated. It must be easy to pull off overhead onstage and also able to conceal the shiny spandex exercise costume worn underneath, which she reveals towards the end of the act. She is wearing trim but athletic-looking sneakers.

Act II: When June emerges from the shower, she is wearing a terry bath/beach shift and is towel-drying her wet hair. Later, when she answers the door to Rushmore, she has changed in the bathroom back to her traveling dress.

SEÑORA VALDEZ

A floral, tropical dress of a self-assertive, flamboyant nature. She shows a great pride of appearance if a little "much." Accessories are prominent.

PORTER

Slightly rumpled, showing effects of tropical heat, the usual black pants. vest, white shirt, and black bow tie.

SMITH

Act I: Dark suit, black shirt, white tie. Briefly, at the beginning of the act, is wearing sunglasses.

Act II: Appears in the same suit, but boxer shorts have replaced suit pants. Later, he reappears in loud, oversized Bermuda shorts.

SCOPEC

Act I: Flashy but well tailored suit, shirt, and tie.

Act II: He has removed his jacket (makes clean-up after the algae drink spill easier).

RUSHMORE

A Hollywood cliché. Loud Hawaiian shirt, white tropical pants and mod sport jacket; a silk tuxedo scarf as the final affectation. At the end of Act I, his trousers come off revealing designer underwear.

KEITH

Sloppy beach shirt, loose trousers, and serious, state-of-the-art sneakers.

PUMPHREY

Wears a conservative summer suit—khaki or blue cord, a white shirt, and a bow tie.

VICTORIA

She is dressed in stylish, sophisticated cruise wear.

PROPERTY LIST

LOBBY

Onstage: Scuba stand. On it: masks, flippers, snorkel tubes, colorful kiddie inner tubes, a grass skirt, and a tropical drink glass with an umbrella and straw. Hassock. On it: Another drink glass. On the floor next to the hassock: June's snap lid hard body suitcase. Bamboo wall-hanging in the shape of a lizard. Wall phone next to the scuba stand.

Offstage: Flash camera with shoulder strap (June); Athletic bag (June); Suitcase identical to June's and filled with cash (Scopec); Revolver (Smith); Eelskin wallet (Smith); Tool belt with bathroom plunger, wrench, and screw driver (Porter); Waiter's tray with glasses (Porter); Video camera (Keith); Business card (Pumphrey); Twenty dollars (Smith)

JUNE'S ROOM

Onstage: Single bed. On it pillow, sheets and a large bedspread that can be hidden under; Table (DR) with curtains around it that can conceal the suitcase. On it: a telephone; Small chair (DL); Bamboo lizard similar to the one in the lobby. This one must be large enough to partly conceal someone.

Offstage: Smith's wallet and gun (Porter); Piña colada glass (Keith); Two large glasses filled with blue green drink (June); Towel (Smith); Tray with drinks (Porter); Celery sticks (June); Dental floss (Pumphrey); Anti-terrorist handbook (Pumphrey); Towel (Pumphrey); Towel (June); Algae mess on Scopec (Water and blue detergent powder)

BATHROOM DOOR
RUSHMORE'S DOOR
ELEVATOR DOORS
JUNE'S DOOR
BEDROOM
HALL
LOBBY

OTHER TITLES AVAILABLE FROM SAMUEL FRENCH

CAPTIVE
Jan Buttram

Comedy / 2m, 1f / Interior

A hilarious take on a father/daughter relationship, this off beat comedy combines foreign intrigue with down home philosophy. Sally Pound flees a bad marriage in New York and arrives at her parent's home in Texas hoping to borrow money from her brother to pay a debt to gangsters incurred by her husband. Her elderly parents are supposed to be vacationing in Israel, but she is greeted with a shotgun aimed by her irascible father who has been left home because of a minor car accident and is not at all happy to see her. When a news report indicates that Sally's mother may have been taken captive in the Middle East, Sally's hard-nosed brother insists that she keep father home until they receive definite word, and only then will he loan Sally the money. Sally fails to keep father in the dark, and he plans a rescue while she finds she is increasingly unable to skirt the painful truths of her life. The ornery father and his loveable but slightly-dysfunctional daughter come to a meeting of hearts and minds and solve both their problems.

OTHER TITLES AVAILABLE FROM SAMUEL FRENCH

TAKE HER, SHE'S MINE
Phoebe and Henry Ephron

Comedy / 11m, 6f / Various Sets

Art Carney and Phyllis Thaxter played the Broadway roles of parents of two typical American girls enroute to college. The story is based on the wild and wooly experiences the authors had with their daughters, Nora Ephron and Delia Ephron, themselves now well known writers. The phases of a girl's life are cause for enjoyment except to fearful fathers. Through the first two years, the authors tell us, college girls are frightfully sophisticated about all departments of human life. Then they pass into the "liberal" period of causes and humanitarianism, and some into the intellectual lethargy of beatniksville. Finally, they start to think seriously of their lives as grown ups. It's an experience in growing up, as much for the parents as for the girls.

"A warming comedy. A delightful play about parents vs kids. It's loaded with laughs. It's going to be a smash hit."
– *New York Mirror*